BOAT RACING

The Second Heat

Ralph DeSilva

SECOND HEAT

Copyright © Ralph DeSilva 2016

Pictures and Written contributions used with permission. When applicable, credit is given to authors, contributors and copyright holders. In some cases credits, dates or other information may not available.

All rights reserved. Except in use of review, no part of this book may be copied or redistributed by photo-copy or any electronic storage or retrieval system without express permission of the author or publisher.

At time of this publication, this book has been submitted for a Library of Congress Control Number, and is subject of Title 17 Copyright Law.

Publication: 2016—1st Edition Print

For information on this book, write:

Ralph DeSilva
P.O. Box
Dallas GA, 3012

Cover Credit: F. Pierce Williams; Eaton, Ohio
Cover Subject: Tim Webber, C – Modified Runabout

SECOND HEAT

SECOND HEAT

Second Heat

This is the second volume written by Ralph DeSilva about his family association with boat racing.

"Now & Then", the first volume was first printed in 2015. These two books depict the history of boat racing which began in an organized way in the 1920's. John DeSilva started his construction of racing boats in 1926. His two sons, William and Ralph continued his design and race boat construction business after WWII.

Unique in that their product was not confined to one racing category, the DeSilva brand covered, at one time or another, successful racing boats in both inboards and outboards.

The author provides a historical sketch of the DeSilva involvement in this fascinating sport. In this second volume I have made an effort to provide an identifying photo of many of the iconic, famous people involved in the sport of boat racing.

SECOND HEAT

Introduction

Most of the photos in this book are full face, purposely so. An action shot on the water may be wonderful and exciting, but gives one no indication of the character creating the action.

These photos enable one to make judgement of the determination and drive that allows them to engage in the dynamic, sometimes dangerous, sport of boat racing.

It has been said that man will often indulge in an esoteric behavior in order to judge himself. It is in the nature of man to compete. We all compete in some manner.

SECOND HEAT

Acknowledgements

The text and photos in this book span a period of over 85 years and to thank everyone who has in some way contributed to "Now & Then" and "Second Heat" would require the size of a phone book.

However, there are those who absolutely must be thanked. First, I must mention that these two books have been self-published. A book devoted to boat racing is absolutely not going to be a best seller. Consequently, a commercial book publisher would be hard pressed to accept such a project.

My grandson, W. Michael DeSilva is a writer of obscure novels. He has knowledge of how a book goes through the process of becoming something that can be sold on Amazon. Without Michael, no book.

Not least, are the many folks who suggested that my age and background would provide a credible book about boat racing.

My daughter, Ann has encouraged, prodded and typed all this verbage, with the technical help of her daughter Jennifer; a super granddaughter. With humor, kindness and grace they have enlightened my life.

Finally, I want to thank all those who, over the past three quarters of a century, have driven DeSilva boats. They and all the other folks who have climbed into a race boat, squeezed the throttle and experienced the unique sensation of going very fast over the water, in a very small boat. Only they truly know how and why boat racing is unique.

Bernie, my friend and volunteer editor, has made certain the text was free of typographical and grammatical errors. Any errors that have slipped through are mine, not of others.

SECOND HEAT

Jerry Waldman

1961 – DePue, Illinois

We met Jerry Waldman at the 1956 Long Beach Alky Nationals. It was not a happy boat race for him. He was following Elmo Belluomini closely in one of the single buoy turns and caught a sponson. The hydro turned over and the outfit close behind made some bodily contact. Jerry ended up in the hospital, where we visited and tried to boost his morale. This adventure did not deter his devotion for boat racing.

He attended all the big outboard boat races as a boat driver and representative of a major spark plug company. He had no peer as a boat driver. Harry Bartolomei once said, "I think I can beat most everyone in boat racing, except of one man – Jerry Waldman. No matter how good I'm going or how good a start, Jerry is always able to win. Thank goodness he only drives hydro, not a runabout."

Jerry Waldman

Photo - Fox

SECOND HEAT

Y-66

We first met Paul Hayes in 1955, at the NOA Nationals, Mt.Carmel, Illinois. At that time he said, "I'm a Willis race boat dealer; and have sold 50 Comet runabouts this year!" He lived in Thayer, Missouri, population of maybe 2000. Now a bit of exaggeration, here and there is to be expected, even in polite society, but that statement was a tad over the edge.

1990 Uruguay, South America
Daniel Cassarino
10'6" Runabout powered by Johnson 15 HP Standard Motor

That Hayes had sold, in one year, a total boat production only possible in two or three years by a relatively small manufacturing company was ludicrous.

But, that was Paul Hayes. He was likeable in the sense that he had no mean intent, he just liked to stretch the truth. He had such a lubricous veracity personality that one had to overlook his Mark Twain statements.

Paul had considerable talent. He could drive a race boat, not a great driver but not bad. His family had money; he operated a motel/café in Thayer. During the early stage of his boat racing career, he drove his own equipment. As he grew older and the outfit became better he most often got other drivers to do the driving. That his equipment was good became obvious, he had no trouble getting top men to drive his boats.

In 1956, Hayes bought one of our runabouts and drove both PR-65 and C service at the Mt. Carmel Nationals. He sent the Speedi-twin to Newton about that time. The PR became history via the German Konig and Quincy/Merc competition, so Paul concentrated on the C service equipment. At one time or another, everyone from Bill Seebold, Jr, Homer Kincaid, Dick Pond to Melvin Cooper drove the equipment with excellent results. In 1956, Hayes and Stan Leavendusky drove to California

SECOND HEAT

for the APBA Nationals at Long Beach. They used Stan's PR and Paul's Speedi-twin on the runabout, no result. They had a few problems. Paul took exception to one thing or another; sweetness and lightness was not the order of the day, but all was forgiven within a short time and they remained friends.

Y 66 Homer Kincaid, F-200 Walter Peterson
The mid-town notorious wind has caught Peterson at start of the C service runabout heat.

Left: 1954, at the North-South Championship, Paul put Melvin Cooper in his runabout. Hayes has his back to the camera – holding the boat.

SECOND HEAT

Stan Leavendusky

1952

He looked like a farmer. He wore farmer's overalls even at the boat races. He was a farmer, he had about 10 acres of peaches and he raised some corn. But, Stan was more than a farmer. He made himself one of the most successful Alky runabout drivers and perhaps one of the best PR and C Service motorman ever. He was big and strong with a pleasing personality. His fierce competitions with the Seebold's are legendary and his association with Paul Hayes of Thayer, Missouri is worth a book or two.

Stan Leavendusky

SECOND HEAT

Long Beach Marine Stadium

1931

Start of a 25 mile marathon. Few rules, race what you bring. The camera looks southeast. A few years later the site was made into the stadium for the 1936 Olympics, Los Angeles.

SECOND HEAT

Yosemite Valley

1927

John DeSilva was involved in the construction of the Ahwahee Hotel, Yosemite Valley in 1927.

The Ahwanhee is the second commercial resort at Yosemite and probably will be the last in this incredible valley. There is no need to describe Yosemite. No one can adequately describe the site. For those who have not placed themselves on the valley floor and looked around, it is very beautiful. It was, of course, crated eons ago by glaciers.

Imagine a young family, father, mother a 5 year old son and another 1 year old. What would be better than to spend a late spring, summer and perhaps part of the fall in one of the most favored spots on Earth and be provided with a good wage, housing and work that one enjoyed.

That is what happened to my father in 1927. The job was to build a grand lodge/hotel to be named the Ahwanhee, an Indian name for a grass covered valley. About 1850, the white men drove Indians out of the valley and named it Yo-sem-ity (a corruption of the Indian O-ham-t-te, Indian name for grizzly bear).

In 1857, the white men farmed a small settlement between the Merced River and the cliffs. The Sentinel Hotel was built on this spot, which became a large village. Probably 1913 was the year autos first entered the valley - coming through a rudimentary trail from Merced.

SECOND HEAT

John DeSilva was born in Bear Valley (several valley's north of Yosemite) and had traveled over the raw, unpaved road to Yosemite in 1918. In 1919, he got hold of a well used Ford Model T and put it into running condition. He fabricated a fancy boat tail behind of the front seat to make a classy roadster which created a stir in the San Joaquin among the younger set.

In early spring of 1927, he learned that the Yosemite park service had contracted with the Camp Curry Co to construct a modern fire-proof hotel in the Valley. Four small hotels had served the public since 1856, but by 1925, only the rustic Sentinel Hotel still existed. Its size, plumbing and basic sewage system was inadequate. The Sentinel, Camp Curry and Yosemite Lodge were fine in the spring, summer and early fall, but totally unsuitable for winter.

A winter resort was needed. The long awaited all-year highway was scheduled for completion in 1926, which would end the sometime isolation caused by snow blocked wagon road.

The US Director of the Interior wanted the construction of an all-weather highway to keep the Valley open through the winter. Old roads were reconstructed, a new park headquarters, and US Post Office were created on the north side of the valley. A first class, modern hotel to house the increasing visitors was the priority.

Construction of the Ahwanhee was to start in the spring of 1926. Architect, Gilbert Underwood, Los Angeles was hired as chief designer and James McLoughlin was named general contractor. Work was to be completed by December 15, 1926 at a total cost of $525,000.

Living accommodations would be made available for construction workers. All the building trades were needed. John DeSilva thought a brief job at one of the world's beauty spots, plus a good wage was not to be missed, so he signed on with the McLoughlin group as a carpenter/foreman.

The living quarters proved to be a cabin at Camp Curry, wood floor, waste high with canvas top. Because the job was expected to be finished prior to arrival of severe weather, the cabin was OK for the family of 2 adults and two small kids.

Because most of the employees had family, a small school was organized. I was enrolled in the kindergarten and spent a summer learning to cope with other kids and how to enjoy the incredible valley.

Early on, we were exposed to one of those life/happenings that one never forgets. Every evening that summer, just after the sun had gone down, something happened that brought the Valley to a standstill.

SECOND HEAT

A woman, with an incredible operatic voice, using a loudspeaker stood atop the massive El Capitan cliff and sang the "Indian Love Call". No music – just her voice. The words vibrated over the Valley in an incredible echo.

When words of the song ended, she gave voice to the melody. If you did not pay attention to the song, her crooning voice as it echoed over the Valley was enough to tell you that this was one of those moments always in memory.

While one was enthralled with all that, a huge bonfire had been lit atop El Capitan and as the girl sang, embers were thrown over the cliff, down the bare rock into the Valley. Cecil B. DeMille could not have topped that spectacle.

****

The valley from Artist Point. One can see the El Capitan cliff on the top, left.

SECOND HEAT

SECOND HEAT

Quincy Welding

2015

In order to accurately provide a correct history of the Quincy Welding contribution to outboard racing, I asked Paul Christner to provide a short history by one of the family.

The following is his contribution to this book. The article was compiled by Art Neadeck, Gene East and Paul Christner.

****

I Remember Chris

By Gene East

As a young lad growing up in La Grange, MO; a small town on the banks of the Mississippi River, about 10 miles upstream from Quincy, IL. I was obsessed with boats and boat racing.

I read every boating magazine I could lay my hands on. I was especially interested in the boat racing articles.

A fishing buddy of my Dad (Jack Bradshaw) took me to my first race in 1956, "The NOA Div-IV World Championships" in Meyer, IL less than 10 miles further upstream from my hometown.

As an avid reader of "Motorboating" and "Powerboat" magazines I knew many of the names of the competitors. I was like a 15 year-old girl at a "Rock concert".

Many of the trailers had decals stating, "Modifications by O.F. Christner" I knew O.F. Christner owned a boat ship in Quincy, but I had no idea what a modification was.

Local boaters were always challenging one another for bragging rights of having the fastest boat in town. That honor was held by our next door neighbor, Eddie Dickerson.

Ed eventually bought a hydro and had it parked in his yard. I've got to get a better look at this!

SECOND HEAT

As I was laying on the ground checking out the "pontoons" (sponsons) under the boat, Virginia (Ed's wife) came outside to make sure I wasn't sabotaging the boat. Later Ed invited me to help him do some testing. Ed later landed a driving job with "Chambers' Equipment Co.", (the Johnson dealership) in Quincy and I started working in the pits for Chambers' racing team at the age of

Above: Quincy's Trailer in front of the shop at 5th and State - 1961

1958

This trailer changed Alky outboard racing in a profound way. Most rigs prior to this innovation carried 3 or 4 boats on a single axle and one or two motors in a comparable box.

A year after the Quincy innovation, it was common to see these huge vehicles in the pits. Boat racing and become a sport that required the usual talent, but also considerable expense.

Expense, plus the ever increasing speed through ever more horsepower (few motor restrictions other than bore and stroke); no weight restriction, has resulted in a sport of decreasing participants.

Perhaps this is all a natural consequences. History is littered with grand enterprises which faded into the past through natural and adverse man made decisions.

17 during the 1958 season.

Chambers quit racing at the end of the season. He found it difficult to justify racing Mercurys & Konigs and selling Johnsons!

Mr. Chambers wasn't especially fond of Mr. Christner and referred to him as "That red-headed

SECOND HEAT

S.O.B."! In addition to being boat & motor competitors, Chambers and Christner were competitors in the construction equipment business.

Anyone familiar with Q.W. boats knows they were painted yellow, but not everyone knows in the early years they were "John Deere" yellow!

During the 1959 season I didn't travel as part of a racing team but I did hangout around Q.W. and did work there as a part time "flunkie". I was still in high school and in the Navy Reserve.

My reserve unit held drills on Monday evening and I usually stopped by Q.W. in uniform prior to going to drills.

Chris used to affectionately call me "Admiral Numb-Nuts".

Not everyone knows the connection Chris, or for that matter, the Quincy community had with the Navy during WWII.

Chris and his wife Vera had 3 small children when the war broke out so he was unlikely to be drafted. However, he did play an important role in the war effort.

Quincy Barge built numerous LCT-6 (landing craft tank) vessels for the U.S. Navy.

These vessels were delivered down-stream to New Orleans where they were shipped to the European and Pacific theaters to put Marine Corps & Army "Boots on the ground".

At that time there was a severe shortage of qualified welders.

Chris is responsible for training and supervising the men and women who built these vessels!

Chris was a native of Mendon, IL; a small town near Quincy.

He was a self-trained mechanic/welder/machinist.

He married Vera Cambridge. They have 7 children; Phyllis, David, Ann, John, Mary, Hilary and Paul.

It has been an honor for me to have been introduced by Vera on many occasions as "Our fourth son"! In fact, Chris treated most of his employees as family. He recognized people make mistakes, but he viewed mistakes as learning opportunities.

What he lacked in formal education he made up for in determination and hard work. He read everything he could find regarding mechanics and engineering.

He may not be officially recognized as an engineer, but there is no question he was a genius!

Chris had his own vocabulary like "Biggen it up" or "Little it down". He used the word "ain't" a lot. His justification was, "A lot of people who ain't saying ain't, ain't eating as good as I am"!

SECOND HEAT

Chris used to carry a 6" scale in his shirt pocket. He could read that scale as accurately as most people can read a micrometer. After his death, the family gave me that 6" scale. I treasure it greatly!

I have many fond memories of my association with Chris during the 11 years he was my employer and the many years he was my friend.

Carl Kiekhaefer despised Q.W. because he felt his Mercury motors were just fine, fresh off the assembly line.

He referred to Quincy Welding as "The Butcher Shop". He even cancelled Quincy Welding's Mercury dealership and cut off access to Mercury parts.

Thanks to Charlie Strang that issue was resolved. Charlie explained how valuable Q.W. was in the testing and evaluation of new parts.

It turned out Mr. K's biggest concern was he wanted top billing.

That is when Merc-Quincy replaced the name Quincy-Merc.

These are just a few of my memories of O.F. Christner. Hope this info helps. There is so much to tell about this amazing man.

Chris and Vera were devoted Catholics. They are buried in the church cemetery in St. Patrick, MO about 35 miles northwest of Quincy.

In all the world there is only one town named "St. Patrick"! How wonderful that someone so unique as Oval Frederic Christner should choose St. Patrick as his final resting place.

1949-1950

Eddie Palmer: Palmer drove the "Miss Quincy", a cloth-decker, B-Utility Runabout built by Arrowhead Boat and Canoe Works in Valley Park, MO. This is the same boat he and Christner took to Lake Alfred FL in 1949 and set a new speed record in the DU Runabout Class with a KG-9 Mercury on it. To make the boat legal, Palmer added heavy oak strips in the bottom of the boat to make it meet the legal weight of 280 pounds.

Sometime in the late 50's or 51, Palmer and Christner split up and Palmer opened his own boat shop. He continued to do custom motor work for local Midwest racers – Junior Wagner and Art Kennedy of St. Louis, MO.

SECOND HEAT

1951-1952

Jim Griffin, Ron Williams, OF Christner, and Freddie Goehl: During this time, Griffin and Williams won several championships for Quincy Welding. This was the time just before the Mark 20H came out. Christner had the old KG-7s running their best. There has been talk that Cecil (Junior) Wagner drove for Christner and Junior's father, Cecil Sr. who owned the foundry where most of the aluminum parts that Christner used were cast. This would include the gravity feed tank on the Mark 20H and the famous Quincy Visu-Matic throttle. Another thing would be the boat number X 1000. Sometime in late 1952 or 1953, Wagner Senior gave Junior and Eddie Palmer a blank check and told them to go find a new runabout. They returned to Quincy with a new DeSilva. The boat was first black with yellow and red numbers. In 1954 the boat was painted the famous black and yellow with Palmer Marine Sales and Service painted on the side. In late 1956 or 1957 Wagner joined the Navy and Christner bought the boat from Wagner Senior. Christner added a V after the X 1000 and this is the start of the number being made famous by Quincy Welding. Quincy Welding's boats remained black and yellow well into the 60's. The boats then became all yellow until the late 60s when the boats were yellow and natural wood and carried the number V 5 that Jim Schoch made famous.

1953-1962

Freddie Goehl, David Christner, Arlen Crouch, Rich Weisenberger, Bob LaLande, Earl Hull, Jim Schoch: This would be a very successful time period for Quincy Welding. In 1955, a young David Christner joined the team. Freddie Goehl returned from the Army. In 1957 Jim Schoch joined the team. At the 1956 NOA Championship in Meyer IL, Freddie won the B runabout. 1957 saw David and Freddie both driving B Runabout DeSilvas with the numbers X 1000-V and 1000-V. In 1959 the Quincy team won World Championships in D Runabout, F Runabout, A Hydro, F Hydro and Unlimited Runabout. 1960 Freddie and Jim won three championships at Lake Ming California. 1961 was another good year. Freddie won F Runabout. Bob LaLande won C Service Runabout at DePue. 1962 Freddie and Arlen left Quincy and went to Texas where they opened a boat ship and David moved to Florida.

1963-1973

SECOND HEAT

Jim Schoch, Earl Hull, Gene East, Frank Volker, Johnny Woods, Jerry Waldman: Early and mid-60s was pretty much the Jim Schoch and Earl Hull show as they won just about everything there was to win. Although he was not employed by Quincy Welding and most thought of him as a Quincy Team driver, Jerry Waldman ran Qunicy engines exclusively. Jerry held many speed records and championships running the Quincy-Merc and Merc-Quincy Loopers. Most old timers remember Gene East as the crew chief for Quincy Welding. Gene did drive a few races and once finished second behind Jim Schoch. Frank Volker also did a little driving but mainly worked on the development of the Looper Exhaust. In 1965 Jim Schoch took a leave of absence to work with the Job Corps in Kentucky where he taught a small engine repair class at a small boys' school. Johnnie Woods from St. Louis, a loyal Quincy customer, took over the driving while Schoch was gone. Schoch returned to Quincy and resumed driving the famous V-5 DeSilva. In all, Schoch won 14 world and national titles while at Quincy welding. Jim quit driving in 1972 and in 1973 he left Quincy Welding. He and Jack Kugler bought Chambers Equipment,

Junior Wagner and Eddie Palmer with first DeSilva runabout brought to Quincy

Junior Wagner & Eddie Palmer

This is the boat that O.F. Christner bought from Wagner's father after he went in the Navy. Dave Christner drove this boat to many wins with the number. X-1000-V

SECOND HEAT

the local Johnson Outboard dealership. Jim later bought out Kugler and still runs the business with his son, Jimmy. Also in 1973, Gene East left Quincy Welding and took a job in St. Louis, MO.

1974 – 1984

Paul Christner, Jack Kugler: After Schoch and East left Quincy Welding, Paul and his father, OF, started working on the Quincy Z Engine as the Looper was on its way out. Paul did most of the driving as they were only running a couple of classes, Kugler drove "the gold Rush" DeSilva with a 350 cc Z Engine on it. Kugler's son, Jeff, set a new record with an M Class Z Engine. In 1984 Christner sold Quincy Welding to Pete Rischar, another old Quincy boat racer. Most of the racing part of the business was bought by Jack Kugler. Kugler and Larry Latta continued with the Z Engine until the VRP and Rossi engines from Italy pretty much took over pro-racing.

This list was put together from old newspapers articles and old race programs that I have. Also old Rooster Tail and Propeller magazines that I got from John Dortch. Most of this information is what I remember growing up in Quincy and living only two blocks from the Quincy Welding shop. I am sure there is some's name that I left out who drove one of Quincy Welding's boats at a race somewhere. This list of names contains the main drivers.

SECOND HEAT

QUINCY WELDING DRIVERS:

Eddie Palmer

Jim Griffin

Ron Williams

OF Christner

Freddie Goehl

David Christner

Arlen Crouch

Rich Weisenberger

Bob LaLande

Earl Hull

Jim Schoch

Gene East

Frank Volker

Johnny Woods

Jerry Waldman

Paul Christner

Jack Kugler

SECOND HEAT

Konig

Berlin was a dismal, broken mess of a city in 1946. It was divided into four sectors where Russian, French, English and Americans controlled in their own unique ways. Berlin was within the Russian zone of divided Germany, but the Yalta agreement had specified that Berlin was to be occupied by the 4 powers until a general agreement could be achieved.

Al Bryant and Mather Byatt, US Army, decided to stay in Europe with the Army of occupation. They both had met and married German girls. Each had jobs that were not unpleasant or strenuous. In fact, they had a good bit of free time.

One early summer day, 1946, they heard some strange noise coming from a nearby canal. They drove their Jeep over to investigate and saw three civilians operating a small outboard boat. Both could speak passable German and quickly learned that this was a test of an outboard motor, which was made by a nearby shop.

Al and Mather were fascinated, what a sport! A very small, very loud motor mounted on a very small boat that went very fast. This was their introduction to boat racing and the Konig motor. Over the next four years both Americans became avid race boat drivers. Mather won a few boat races that were held in western Germany. In fact, Mather set a couple of European speed records, all with the Konig motor.

When the time came for the two Americans to return to the US, they suggested that the Konig Company export their motors to the US; they would do the importing. Al moved to Atlanta in 1950 and sold a few Konig motors. He started an air conditioning business which occupied most of his time and he had no storage space for racing motors. Mather also returned to Georgia. He suggested that they ask Al's sister's husband, Scott Smith, Dallas, be a dealer and store the incoming motors. Scott operated a general hardware store and had considerable family real estate around Dallas, Georgia.

Over a short time, Scott became the sole American importer of the Konig motor. He was probably bored with the hardware business and the Konig effort promised to be an exciting and glamorous activity. His promotion of the Konig, from 1952, was basic to Konig success in the US. It was also basic that over the years, the Konig racing motor proved to be a great product. Scott, over the years, is thought to have provided financial support to the Konig factory.

SECOND HEAT

Rudolf Konig (1894-1982) founded the firm in 1927. He retired in 1979. The company started with the design and construction of outboard motors; in 1932 produced a stern drive. In 1938, Rudolf designed a 3 cylinder radial engine which was remarkable and became their mainstay product. The engine was designed to compete against the very fast Italian Laros motor.

WWII turned their shop into the production of storm boat motors for the Wehrmact. Their company building was destroyed by the  Allied bombing, and their market for boat motors was destroyed. Very slowly the firm put rebuilt their manufacturing capability and made the effort to regain its pre-war status. Sales came back slowly. They made an entry into the ultra-light airplane market. Their pre-war 3 cylinder motor, with considerable improvement, was their major product and the motor that enabled a successful entry into the post-war American race boat market.

Dieter Konig came to the US in 1954. He ably demonstrated his motors by driving them at championship regattas. His single cylinder 7 CID (M class) motor obsoleted the old two cylinder Evinrude motor with remarkable ease.

He had a tougher time with a larger horsepower classes. But the demise of the KR, SR and PR was only a matter of time. His competition in America came from the Yamato Alky motors and the

SECOND HEAT

American Quincy/Mercury. During the '80's and '90's, the Italian Rossi and VRM provided serious competition in the field of outboard and motorcycle racing motors.

Dieter was fatally injured while testing an ultra-light aircraft in 1994. His son, Peter, tried to carry on, but was unable to compete with the superior Italian motors and closed the shop in 1998.

Scott Smith, Deiter Konig and wife Eleanora

Scott Smith & Deiter Konig
1955
Testing in Florida, prior to attending the upcoming NOA National Championship at Mt. Carmel, Illinois.

SECOND HEAT

John & Jack Maypole

1957 – Mt. Carmel, IL

In 1931, Jack and his father had made a long difficult trip from Chicago to Lake Merritt, Oakland, CA where he won the B Hydro National Championship. In this photo, 26 years later, Jack and his son, John are trying to win another.

Photo-Fox

Jack Maypole & son

SECOND HEAT

Son of a Plumber
Essay by Alan Ishii

Richard V. Collins was born in San Diego, CA, son of a plumber. Growing up on the mean streets of a harbor town, he had no choice but to be tough, equipped with only a 4th grade education. His childhood friend was William Boyd. Known in the movies as Hopalong Cassidy. RV was nicknamed "Spitty" for obvious reasons. Evolved into "Smitty" as he was to become known. He moved north to Los Angeles to open a plumbing business and machine ship. Later, closing the plumbing business to concentrate on boat building. His business was named "Collins Boat Works".

He began outboard racing at the sports' inception. Driving an F Class runabout with 4-60 power. He was sponsored by Sam Mosher, founder of Signal Oil. Smitty branched out to midget car racing, a very popular sport in urban Los Angeles. Smitty did not drive the cars. Drivers included Rex Mayes, Spider Lockhart and Ralph DePalma. Racing was a popular sport prior to arrival of professional teams in Los Angeles. There were wooden tracks as well as those on dirt. Boat racing was highlighted by the Hearst Regatta, held at Long Beach Marine Stadium which was constructed for the 1932 Olympic rowing even. The race, sponsored by Hearst Newspapers was possibly the premier sporting even in Los Angeles at that time. Smitty was featured in many publications, including Life Magazine. He mounted a torpedo on his F Runabout to support the war effort. Perhaps the idea for PT boats?

Smitty was very successful in the marine business prompting an offer to become

R. V. Collins, the reigning Class "F" National Professional Outboard Motorboat Champion, set a new world's speed record in five miles of competition at Lake Elsinore in California on July 2nd 1933. He drove his Signal "Tarzan" boat with an OMC 4-60 racer around the course at an average speed of 46.7 mph (the old record was 44.9 mph). This photo was taken at the Lake Los Angeles Motor Boat Speedway where he races nearly every Sunday. Note how the boat is essentially out of the water except for the fin on the bottom.

SECOND HEAT

the west coast distributor for Mercury Outboards. He later had a dispute with Carl Kiekhaufer regarding the cosmetics of his building leading to Elgin Gates obtaining the distributorship. His grandsons, Richie and Ripper, raced the Mercurys with Collins built boats. Although having a swarthy reputation as a young man, he was an affable philosopher and boat builder when I met him. He was in failing health. Diabetes was the culprit. He was a double amputee who has perhaps 50 daily heart attacks. He was stricken with San Joaquin Valley fever, a lung fungus that left him with only a partial lobe of one lung after 3 surgeries. His son, the doctor, performed a tracheotomy at his home to save his father's life.

Smitty continued building boats. Everything from yachts to racing boats. Smitty and his wife, Millie, were blessed with two children, a boy and a girl. Tragedy occurred when the daughter fell victim to illness because a physician was not available. Smitty and Millie decided to do everything they could to encourage their son, Rich to become a doctor. Smitty continued to build racing boats. Boat building was this therapy. The last National Championship for a Collins boat was in 1972 in 250 Runabout. He was building a hydro when he died in 1974. A Picklefork 125 and B Stock. The Butts Aerowing was described to him. He thought that the design was innovative and indeed a safety feature. It was perhaps his best boat? RV enjoyed teaching others. Among them Ernie Dawe. Today builder of the successful Dawecraft Boats. Sean McKean won the first of his many championships in a Collins clone. In spite of lack of formal education, RV was excellent with his design and technique. RV battled diabetes every day of his life. Yet, life was good. It was not the life that makes the person. It is the person that makes the life.

Rich did indeed become a doctor. Completing undergraduate studies at UCLA. He was a fun loving fellow whose grades were not acceptable to local medical schools. He was accepted at George Washington University in St. Louis. Internship provided an excellent education in emergency trauma treatment. He received experience in violent wounds, which would later become invaluable to his medical career. Doctor Collins was also a Navy physician. He served twice in the Korean was. One is a MASH unit and another on a ship. He and his wife, Alice, had three children, Richie, Ripper and bonnie. Bonnie followed her father into a medical career, practicing medicine in the state of Washington. Richie and Rip both raced A class hydro and runabouts. Racing is indeed in the family bloodlines. Dr. Collins became a respected obstetrician and gynecologist. His patients included wives and mothers of boat racers.

SECOND HEAT

Dr. Collins was on the faculty of USC Medical Center. When Alex Pugh ruptured his spleen in DePue, the doctor treating him in emergency was one of his students. Dr. Collins was a big sports fan with season tickets to USC, UCLA and the Lakers. He was friends with sports surgeons, Dr. Kerlan and Dr. Jobe. However, boat racing was his recreational life. He was very successful with his boats driven by Ted May and others. He later began the entry level class today known as K Pro. Many times at races he helped with injuries. Memorable was a horrible accident in Sparks, Nevada. Frank Zorkan was injured riding in a F runabout. Dr. Collins held his shoulder together in the ambulance. Frank loved boat racing more than anyone. He sent his wife, Wanda, back to the pits to find a driver to substitute for him in his B hydro. Is that devotion?

Lifelong friends with RV was George Ishii. George too loved speed. Began by taking the fenders off his mothers' car to run time trials at Muroc Dry Lake. He too became attracted to the popular outboard racing. Running Jacoby Class B and C Hydroplanes. He was third in the contentious B Hydroplane class at the 1939 Hearst Regatta. Unfortunately, the advent of was and internment halted his racing career until racing with his son in the 1960's and 70's. George had worked for Riley Carburetors after WWII. He tuned the arbs for Bill Vukovich's midget every week. The advent of fuel injection led to the demise of Riley's business. George opened a machine shop in 1953. The business is now operated by his sons. Visitors to his machine shop include Lee Sutter, Ron Anderson, Bob Martin, Bob Weikert, Jim Rhea, Jim McKean, Ralph and Bill DeSilva. He and RV were friends until George's death. RV and George built a 18' sportfisher in the 1970's.

Racing was paramount to the Collins and Ishii families. They thought they had control over the boats, when in reality; the boats had control over them.

SECOND HEAT

Fred Miller

We sold a B stock runabout to Paul Kalb in 1969. Delivery was made at the Great Colorado River National Marathon Championship. He arrived with Fred Miller, who brought his own B stock outfit. He said, "I'm going well and expect to win." He had been doing well in mid-west competition and was confident the coast competition would be no problem. However, his motor refused to cooperate and gave up shortly after the start.

At that time, Fred was a Michigan real estate agent. Over the years, we heard that Miller had become a real force in boat racing, as a competitor, official, promoter and subsequently a race manager for Outboard Motor Corporation.

It was not until 1984 that we sold Miller a race boat. He had met Dave Bryan at the 1983 APBA National Convention who told Fred that he was having success with our C stock runabout. This comment resulted in an order from Miller. Subsequent results were impressive. Sometimes with his own power plant, but perhaps more often with borrowed motors and propellers, he won an impressive number of championships and competition records. Fred Miller is currently living the good life in Tennessee and promotes a few OPC events.

Fred Miller

SECOND HEAT

NOA National Championship
Knoxville, TN

1951

This was the only race attended by Fred Jacoby, Sr. where we met. He said, "I'm getting too old to travel to these events!" He may have been in his 90's at that time, but seemed to be spry and heathly.

Right Fred Jacoby North Beren N.J.
Left Ralph Tatum Jackson MS.

SECOND HEAT

Randolph Hubbell

About 1955

This is a relatively rare photo of a remarkable man. After serving as an officer in the Army Air Force during WWII, Pep moved from somewhere in the east (Ohio, I think) where the family had a loan company. He did not want to spend the rest of his life loaning money at interest, so he moved his wife and two daughters to Rosemead, CA. Rosemead is an L.A. suburb on the east side. We met Pep early on in his career as a motor manufacturer.

He lived in a mobile home for a short time, until he purchased property on Rosemead Blvd for a machine shop. His effort was remarkable. As a high class machinist, he began to make or reproduce parts and build complete new PR-65 and SR motors. He made lower units for the 4-60, PR's, SR's and KR's. He did everything! He literally carried Alky boat racing on his back until the Quincy-Merc and Konig motors arrived in the mid '50's.

Later in life, he became a champion discus athlete and held several records in the Senior Track & Field Association, USA.

Pep and I surprised ourselves by discovering that he had spent a little time at the headquarters of a 9th Air Force unit stationed out of Oxford, England about 10 miles off the road to High Wycomb, where I served for some months prior to the Normandy invasion.

Randolph Hubbell

Photo - Fox

SECOND HEAT

Dick Pond

1965

Dick Pond began his boat racing career in the late '50's, out of Keokuk, Iowa. No one drove an outboard race boat better.

His performance at the NOA National Championships in 1960 at St. Paul on the Mississippi, was legendary.

Bill Tenney had two hydros entered in the B hydro class – powered by his Anzani motor. One to be driven by Dale Kaus, Minnesota, the other by Pond. Dick arrived late. Someone had made his bail…he had been jailed on an excessive speeding charge.

He was placed into the larger of the two boats for a short test. He returned to the pits and asked for a smaller prop – he wanted more RPM. Tenney refused – they had been testing for two days and Kaus had things going OK. After a bit of argument and discussion, Pond prevailed. Tenney knew it would be best make his driver confident and happy.

There were too many boats and elimination heats were required. Pond led into the first turn. The hydro turned inside the middle buoy. He snapped around said buoy, which put him almost last in the 10 boat field. He had expected the boat to slide in a usual manner…it did not. Our boat had been designed to cope with the expected Mississippi water conditions and we had a boat that was very directional. The boat turned well.

It is not often that one will see a boat overtake 7 or 8 in the short interval of a 4 lap event. Dick finished 2nd in the heat – the last place in which to qualify.

Pond got a good start in the first heat of the final and won – no problem. In the second, someone crowded him at the start – he was unable to get into a good position and arrived at the first turn in 4th place. He placed second to Bill Seebold, Jr. (Konig). His total points for the two heats made him champion. Kaus placed third.

We were delighted. Our hydros had won 3 straight NOA National Championships – Kaus two and Pond one.

And, at St. Paul, we had received our 15 minutes of fame (15 seconds actually)! A CBS reporter asked Pond – "who built your boat?" Pond patted the hydro and said, "the DeSilva brothers of Los Angeles, CA".

SECOND HEAT

Photo - Fox

Dick Pond

SECOND HEAT

Orlando Torgiani

1952

Orlando Torgiani was a cotton farmer who owned several thousand acres in the flat productive land around Buttonville, near Bakersfield, California.

He began boat racing after WWII. Orlando could do anything and everything on the farm. He could drive, maintain and repair all the light and heavy machinery needed on such a farm; he had discretionary time. After the various crop was planted, only an occasional irrigation was necessary.

Lake Buena Vista was just a few miles away. At that time, the Kern River was not controlled as it is today and overflow/flooding had created this rather big lake on the San Joaquin Valley west side. So one had plenty of water in which to play with boats.

His specialty was the Johnson KR Class A (15 CID) alky racing motor. He probably was as good as Vincent, Draper or Blakenstein insofar as being a KR expert. He proved this time after time for about 10-12 years at the National Championships held yearly.

The photo is of Orlando, about 40 years after winning A hydro at the NOA Championships Lake Village, Arkansas in 1952.

Photo - Fox

SECOND HEAT

SECOND HEAT

Joel Thorne

1935

Joel Thorne started outboard racing while a student at Rutgers University in the '30's.

In 1934, he won the prestigious Townsend High Point Trophy, while driving A, B and C hydro. He later switched to auto racing, everything from a 4-60 powered midget to the Indianapolis 500. He never won the Indy, but was usually up front – 9th (1935) and 5th (1940).

Joel Thorne New Rochell NY. Class B

SECOND HEAT

Ted May
1969

Ted May was a mystery man. No one knew much about him and how he made a living. But he was always around, at most every big race event.

We first ran into Ted at Lake Los Angeles (The Puddle), where he did crazy things with a home built Popular Mechanic's type puddle-jumper powered with a 10 horse fishing motor.

He quickly graduated into various stock category race boats. A short time later he had some Alky equipment. He drove anything and everything – with abandon.

Ted was hired to teach the two Nordskog boys how to boat race; off and on he drove for the motor factories. He was lead driver in several Paris 6 Hour events for OMC. He drove for Doc Collins – they won NOA class A (250 CID) Runabout National Championship at Midland, Michigan in 1962.

I once asked him how he was able to attain the top job with all those talented folks. He replied, "I always told them I was going faster than my speedometer indicated!"

SECOND HEAT

Alan Ishii

Alan Ishii has been involved in boat racing all his life. His father, George, started driving an outboard hydro in the Los Angeles area, during the '30's.

Alan grew up in that mileau. He knew and knows everybody. He began driving a race boat at any early age. His father operated a general machine shop located in downtown LA. Their boat racing equipment was first class.

The APBA Stock program came along at an ideal time for Alan. He was a boat race veteran, of an ideal age, possessed keen eyesight with small weight and stature. Alan was in immediate demand as a driver for those who had equipment but for one reason or another could not themselves drive a boat.

Alan drove, stock and Alky, for about 10-12 years. He was well known and respected up and down the west coast, in the mid-west and wherever one is likely to race on the water.

SECOND HEAT

Western Spruces

We have often been asked:

What wood do you use for your boats? Engleman Spruce is a term not generally known by box stores or lumber yards.

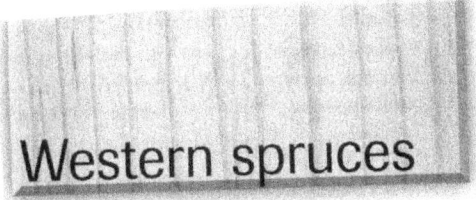

Western spruces

Two major spruces are found in the western forests of the United States. Engelmann spruce (*Picea engelmannii*) is found throughout the Rocky Mountains, from Alberta to Arizona. It's named after George Englemann, who discovered this species in the mid-1800s.

Sitka spruce is found primarily within 50 miles of the Pacific Coast, from Alaska to northern California. The name comes from Sitka Island, where the tree was discovered in 1892; Sitka spruce is also Alaska's state tree.

Spruce trees are one of the largest trees in the western forests, often reaching 175 feet in height and 3 to 6 feet in diameter. They may live 700 years. A record-sized tree in Oregon is nearly 17 feet in diameter and more than 215 feet high.

For their weight, the spruces are exceptionally strong. Hence, spruce has been used for airplanes, including propellers, where high strength was required, but weight needed to be as low as possible. (Note: Howard Hughes' "Spruce Goose" airplane used primarily birch.)

Thin panels of Sitka spruce are noted for their very good sound resonance. Hence, they are preferred for quality piano sounding boards. Spruce is also used for other stringed instruments, such guitars.

Other uses for spruce include furniture, millwork, cabinets, sailing ship masts and other components. ◄

(Wood from these two trees is nearly identical in processing and properties; Englemann is slightly lighter weight and weaker. Data here is for Sitka.)

Density. Sitka spruce weighs about 27 pounds per cubic foot.

Drying. Spruce dries very easily, but lumber intended for remanufacturing should not be dried under 9 percent MC or the wood can become too brittle when machining. Shrinkage in drying is 3 percent (quartersawn) to 6 percent (flatsawn).

Gluing and machining. Gluing is excellent. Machining is excellent if tools are sharp and any machine pressures are not high. Chipped grain is common when machining close to a knot.

Stability. Spruce is fairly stable, requiring about 4 percent MC change to have a size change of 1 percent (tangential direction or the width of flatsawn lumber). For quartersawn lumber, a 7 percent MC change will cause a 1 percent width change (radial direction).

Strength. Spruce is moderately strong for its size, but very strong for its weight. The strength (MOR) is 10,200 psi; stiffness is 1.57 million psi; and hardness is 510 pounds.

SECOND HEAT

Congress & Laurel

1933

We were living in Pacific Grove, in a duplex on the corner of Congress and Laurel. I remember that because my mother made Bill and me place the location firmly in mind case of emergency.

One day, I was near the garage when a passing older man stopped at a pile of wood lying about and said, "Young man, do you know what that wood is? It's a rare and beautiful wood – Mahogany." I replied, "Yes, my father builds boats out of it. We burn this scrap in the fireplace."

The pile consisted of mostly 5/16" planking from 6" to 8" wide. It was used for bottom planking and sides. There were some odd size material mostly milled stock. My father purchased this Philippine mahogany from big lumber companies in San Francisco and Oakland. Price of mahogany, at that time, was about $.07-$.08 per foot, milled. At that price, one could burn the scrap.

The old man shook his head and walked away.

Bass Lake, California

1950
Ken Jolly, Burbank, CA about to get wet; start of 2 man "F" runabout as they approach starting line.

SECOND HEAT

Pride of the Navy - Again

This is probably the only existing photo of the torpedo boat built by John DeSilva that shows the boat under way with the use of its own power.

It would seem that the boat is powered by two inboard motors in front of each driver/mechanic. However, the propulsion came from a Johnson P-50 outboard motor on each transom, under the rear cowling. This was done to keep the project cost down to a minimum. However, this nearly proved disastrous. At the time, the electric start outboard motor was almost unknown and very unreliable. They tried to put a mechanic in each rear cowl, but that did not work due to trapped smoke created by the motor exhaust.

However, the movie did not require the boat to be shown moving over the water except toward the end when it made a demonstration torpedo run for the Navy brass. That problem was solved by using a fast high powered harbor launch which pulled the torpedo boat via a long cable at dusk.

It was only a B movie, a fantasy, $.75 to see only a slight bit of nonsense.

SECOND HEAT

FLASH   FLASH   BULLETIN   FLASH   FLASH

Outboard Racing passed a milestone early February 1983, when Harry Bartolomei, Hayward, California, streaked through the Modesto Kilo trials at a World Record shattering 102.004 mph.

The long sought after Outboard limited cubic displacement Runabout record "Ton" was achieved with a German Konig 40 cubic inch alky powered De Silva 13'6" KR Professional Division racing runabout.

The 100 mph Outboard Runabout mark has been attained with various Unlimited size motors, but Bartolomei's is the first achieved by a Limited displacement motor. The 40 Cubic Inches or 700 cc translates to four cylinders, with a bore of about 1 3/4" each, whereas most of the Unlimited motors are in the area of 150 Cubic Inches or about 4 times the size of the Konig class D motor. Of course, the konig motor spins at something like 12,000 rpm, with a propeller of about 7" x 12, which produces both amazing speed and acceleration relative to size.

Race drivers over the last decade have speculated about the Outboard Runabout "TON" and who would be the driver to do it. It is fitting that Harry Bartolomei be Professional Outboard standard bearer, for he is a veteran of over 25 years in the Sport.

Harry has an amazing record of achievement in Boat Racing - numerous National Championships and other World records in practically every class of Alky Outboard racing. We have always recognized Harry as a Driver and Mechanic of rare talent.

Harry has the ability to demonstrate his capabilities - instead of merely displaying "potential". It is always a privilege to see and acknowledge excellence. Too often, one merely settles for the easy way and thus mediocrity.

-30-

Speed	-	102.004 MPH
Location	-	Modesto, California (Turlock Resv.)
Date	-	12 February 1983
Motor	-	Konig (German)
Class	-	Outboard Professional Division 700 cc - 40 cubic inches D class
Boat	-	De Silva KR 13'6" - 1979 Model DSACDR110679
Owner - Driver	-	Harry Bartolomei

SECOND HEAT

Ralph Donald

1957 – Konig Motor

There is a school of philosophy that says, "Less is more". Here is a boat race example of that idea.

In the early days, boat speed was not what it is today. Very small boats of questionable stability were not considered objectionable. However it took a brave man to master a runabout such as the one in this photo.

SECOND HEAT

Crack Up - Two boats Indiana boats Class B runabouts 1954

SECOND HEAT

Melvin Cooper

Class C Hydro – Konig motor middle of a turn

SECOND HEAT

Left to Right Kneeling Clay Pettefer, Harry Demski, Bill Holland, Dub Parker, Deanie Montgomery. Standing L to R O.B. Ayler Bud Jones, Mel Callaway, Wally Adams, Bill Tenney,

SECOND HEAT

D Runabout

Outboard

VOLUME 1   MAY, 1946   **No. 7**

Official publication of National Outboard Drivers Association, Inc., 113 St. Clair Ave., N.E., Cleveland 14, Ohio. Published monthly. Mailed to all members of the National Outboard Drivers Association, a national organization of outboard owners, dealers, outboard enthusiasts, outboard clubs, yacht clubs, boat clubs, athletic clubs, and manufacturers. Obtained by membership subscription and by direct subscriptions.

PISTONS

Sand-cast, heat-treated, accurately machined pistons for 4-60 motors

Also high dome racing pistons for service "C" motors

CLYDE WISEMAN

CLEVELAND WIRE PRODUCTS CO.

1383 East 92nd Street   Cleveland, Ohio

Phone: CEdar 7493

WILSON MARINE SALES AND SERVICE

170 TERRACE   BUFFALO 2, NEW YORK

EASTERN STATES DISTRIBUTORS FOR

Ace-O-Speed Racing Fuel

5 or 55 gallon lots — Order now

WHOLESALE DISTRIBUTORS FOR

Perfect Circle Rings

Write for information

Jim Wilson   Ken Wolff

Two Powerful Fuel Concentrates & Octanizer released by rescinded government restriction order October 5, 1945. Now compounded into

POWER MIST - SPITFIRE - BLUE BLAZER

DEALER'S STOCK NOW AVAILABLE

FUEL FACTS, FORMULAS AND TESTING INFORMATION SENT UPON REQUEST

FRANCISCO LABORATORIES

3787 Griffith View Drive — Los Angeles 26, California

Propeller Repitching   Propeller Rebalancing

MARINE PROPELLER SPECIALIST

FRANK M. PARK

211 S. Washington St.

New Bremen, Ohio

Propeller Refinishing - Special Propellers to Order

B & C CRANKSHAFTS   B & C TANK BRACKETS

B & C CYLINDER BRACKETS

B Heads - Bronze Swivel Brackets - Steering Brackets

Pistons - Cylinders Ground and Chromed

Detroit Outboard Specialties

15133 KERCHEVAL AVE.   DETROIT 30, MICH.

SECOND HEAT

Above: Fred Mulky – C.57
Below: Lake Village Arkansas - 1952

SECOND HEAT

John Woods & Momma Smith

1965

Mrs. Smith, wife of Alan Smith, renowned maker of racing propellers, often attended boat races with her husband. In the photo she is handing a homemade delicacy to John.

When not making money as a St. Louis stock broker, John was deeply involved in boat racing – he enjoyed the spe and competition. John was such a fine boat competitor that he was often invited to drive for the famed Quincy/Merc racing team. ed

SECOND HEAT

Jack Corner & Ray Harris

1948

Long Beach Marine Stadium

Jack Corner is taking a photo of Ray Harris about a pass a 4-60 competitor as they go into the first turn.

The cab over was the 4th boat that design built by DeSilva. All the oil derricks are now gone. Apartment houses and some commercial structures have taken their place. The camera is looking east.

SECOND HEAT

This is not fair! I took a bath 2 weeks ago I don't have any soap and the water is colder than I like.

SECOND HEAT

380 George May/ 560C Ted May A Hydro

Sometimes it's best to take a dive (Old boxing proverb)

SECOND HEAT

McAlester, Oklahoma
NOA Nationals 1958

1958 was a pretty good in the US. Business was, in general, O.K., manufacturing had supplied the needs pent up by the scarcity produced by WWII and our exports were creating a robust economy.

There were, however, one or two problems folks were concerned about. One was that our automobile industry needed a serious shakeup. The cars offered by the Big 3 were largely junk. Bad design and shoddy construction were the norm. Planned obsolesce was their moto.

We purchased a station wagon to attend the upcoming Oklahoma NOA Nationals in July 1958. We left LA late one afternoon and headed for Needles on Highway 66. I was driving sometime after midnight out of Wilkinsburg when the car's headlights went out. We were out in the middle of nowhere, no traffic, no lights, no nothing. Fortunately there was enough moonlight and very little oncoming traffic, so we limped into Williams and found the Chrysler dealership. They found a short in the electrical system. No charge, we were under new car warranty.

Off we go into New Mexico, no electrical power going into Tucumcari, so another 2 hours under warranty. On to Oklahoma City for another 2 hours under warranty. We finally arrived in McAlester, OK where by this time the car problem was a major concern. None of the auto mechanics knew what the basic problem was. They gave us lights.

On the trip back to California, we stopped in Amarillo for gas. Bill began a conversation with the attendant, an older man. "I know what your problem is, we run into that all the time". You have a junction box between the car battery and your light system. If the battery line is not disconnected when a new fuse is installed, a failure will occur. The whole junction box system should be redesigned.

At the next oncoming Chrysler dealership, we had them follow this procedure and we had no further problem. The station wagon was replaced by a different brand soon after our return to California.

The McAlester Nationals was also noteworthy for another reason. Soon after arrival we were advised that the Stockyard Café was the best place to eat. McAlester, at the time, had a population of about 15,000-20,000. Big enough to support a few gastronomical outlets other than the usual fast food providers. Sadly, there were not, the Stockyard Café was the best available.

SECOND HEAT

However, this was not bad. Bill and I, over the years, had occasion to visit a good many sections of the US and sampled cooking in most all of its flavors.

Nowhere, no place, before or since have we ever had steak as good as those provided at the Stockyard Café, McAlester, Oklahoma in 1958. They had, on the menu, steak for two $5.00 each. Cut of sirloin about 8" long and 1" thick, done to perfection, your request, great fresh salad, your choice of 3 or 4 side dishes plus iced tea, coffee or soft drink; served ice cold in a 10oz glass. Yes, I said $5.00 for two. I forgot the dessert, apple or key lime pie or fresh peach (seasonal) with ice cream (flavor your choice). I repeat, steak for two $5.00. After the third day and a repeat of all this, the very pleasant middle-aged waitress without asking, brought the drinks and food. When asked about the Café and how well they were doing, she replied, "We have been here since I was a little girl. We got folks from all over Oklahoma. We even have the Governor in here once in a while. Will Rogers, when he comes back to Oklahoma, comes in and has a steak."

SECOND HEAT

What do we do now?

SECOND HEAT

David Livingston

1952

We first met David Livingston when he was a high school student at Lake Village Arkansas. This was in 1952.

His speech was pure Arkansas argo and a little hard to follow by those not acquainted with its lilt and inflections. The kid could drive a boat. He and his father had acquired a Newton C Service motor and their hydro and runabout were near unbeatable.

The next year, 1953, the NOA Nationals were again at Lake Village. David had gone off to college and what a change in speech. His local accent was gone, he spoke pure unaldultrated American-English. And, their boat equipment was once again superior. He won both C Service Runabout and Hydro Championships.

Dorothy Mayer appeared at many National Championship after WWII. She drove an M hydro and perhaps a KR.

David Livingston Lake Village AR.
Dorthy Mayer Collage Point LI NY.

SECOND HEAT

Doug Fonda

About 1936

This is a rare photo of one of the "giant" outboard race drivers from the "thirties". He was reported to be a man of Wall Street, a banker. It is rather unusual for a man with such an occupation to find time to participate in a sport that demands considerable time and mechanical expertise.

He apparently had both because his record over a lengthy career as a boat race driver was one of noteworthy success.

Photo - Fox

Doug Fonda

SECOND HEAT

Don Whitefield

1939

One had to be small in weight and stature to satisfactorily compete in the midget class. Don Whitefield may have been of small size but he was a giant as a "Midget" driver. He dominated the class for a generation.

Don Whitefield Midget Class National Champion 1939 Montclair NJ.

SECOND HEAT

Dick Neal

1940

Dick Neal had a long and varied career in outboard racing. He started out as a driver, became an absolute man-to-beat. He worked hard to become a leading motor "hop-up" artist.

His boat and motor shop in Kansas City on Troost Avenue, became a mecca for the racing fraternity during the '40's and '50's.

He hired Shorty Fillinger to build a line of hydroplanes, which dominated boat racing for 25 years.

Y 50 Dick Neal

SECOND HEAT

James Aderholt

1970

Alabama has never been a hotbed for boat racing, although the state has a plethora of water venues. However, James Aderholt, driver par exellance, has always represented the state in an exemplary manner.

An auto painter, he was adversely effected by one of the exotic paint finishes. At the hospital they told him, "…one more trip here, for the same reason, it will be a DOA." He changed occupation. At the moment he still drives an Alky hydro

Photo - Fox

SECOND HEAT

Dale Robertson

1966

We sold Dale Robertson, Michigan, a 13' flat deck roundabout in 1966.

Dale drove two classes, PR and C Service. His Speedi-twin motor was pretty good, not Newton quality, but close. The PR needed work but it did not matter, he always had fun and was involved.

Photo-Fox

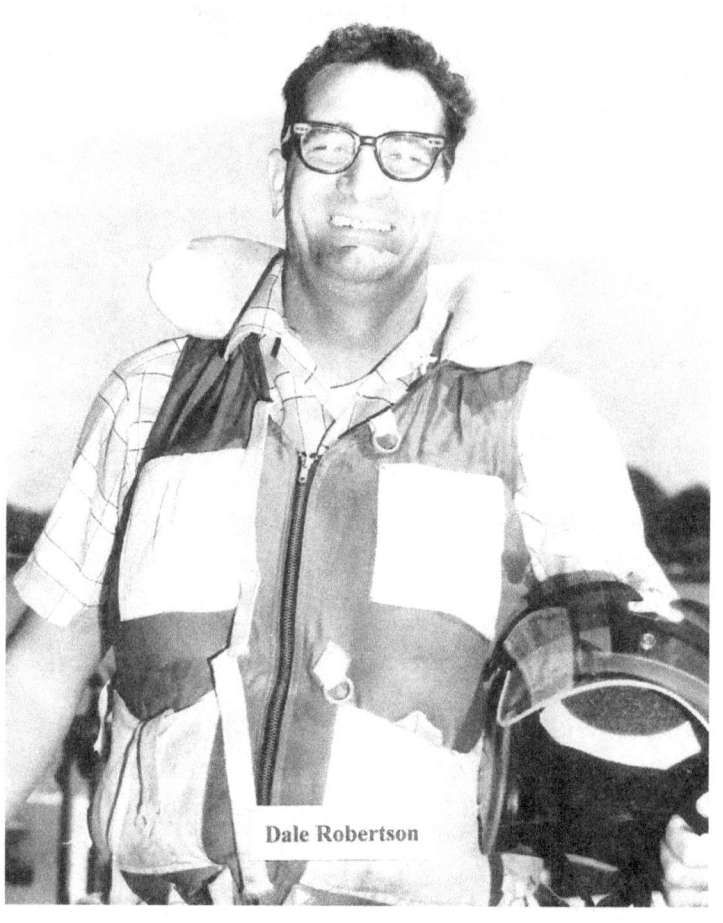

SECOND HEAT

Harry Vogts

1963

Harry Vogts was a veteran boat race driver. He began racing prior to WWII, drove PR and 4-60 hydros. Harry was a tough competitor. He drove to win and was rarely "out-of-the-money".

He had a large industrial foundry and had everything necessary to win a boat race.

Photo-Fox

Harry Vogts Madison WI.

SECOND HEAT

Bedford Davie

1938

Bedford Davie was one of the contingent of young drivers who entered outboard racing in the mid '30's. His interest and affection was for the large motors especially the 4-60. In 1987, Mr. Davie, Arizona got hold of a PR-65 and had us build a Neal Banjo hydro which he wanted to set some records and win a race or two.

The effort was not successful. He could not find an enthusiastic driver who put the outfit into competitive trim.

**Bedford Davie Jacoby Boat
Record 71+ Green Pond NJ.**

SECOND HEAT

Arthur Kennedy

1954

Arthur Kennedy, St. Louis, owned both modified and alky equipment. He did not campaign nationally. He was active in the early '50's – up and down the Mississippi River Valley.

Photo – Fox

SECOND HEAT

Robert McGinty

1952

Robert McGinty drove Harry Marioneoux's Alky equipment. That they did well was no surprise – Harry was a successful Louisiana oil man and Bob was an experienced and very capable driver. In addition, they had the personal supervision of Allen Smith – Shreveport's great contribution to outboard racing during the '30's, '40's, '50's and '60's.

Photo - Fox

SECOND HEAT

Boots Murphy

1954

He can be seen in one of James Stewart's westerns. He and his wife "Boots" who was not an actress arrived in LA after the war, bought a home just north of Hollywood Blvd and began boat racing.

Lou was the only driver to use a Willis runabout while living on the west coast.

Boots was a very successful midget hydro racer who won many races around the country in the early 1950's.

Photo - Fox

MOVIE STAR....BOOTS MURPHY AND HUSBAND LOU, HOLLYWOOD, CALIFORNIA

SECOND HEAT

Vic Scott

1940

This pre-war driver had a reputation. To beat him was a bottle. His equipment was the best – a Draper PR and latest hydro from the Jacoby factory.

He retired to the South and often appeared at the frequent driver conventions promoted by Claude Fox.

Vic Scott

SECOND HEAT

Doug Creech

Doug Creech lived on the east coast, Charlotte, NC. He operated a successful motorcycle business. He found time to travel the US both in the pre-war '30's into the hectic '50's era. He campaigned some very good A-B-C class hydroplanes.

At Salton Sea one year, in one of the early '50's, he established several new competition records. He frequently appeared on the west coast, all the way from New Bern, North Carolina. He was a friendly person, but a tough, formidable competitor on the water.

Photo - Fox

Doug Creech 1952 Mischey Vincent Trophy

SECOND HEAT

Byron Sonny King III

1950

Bryon King, Orlando, Florida, had a very hot PR motor which powered a great performance at the APBA Alky Nationals at Lake Alford, FL.

He won the class C Championship and set a kilo record of 56+mph. He had removed the cavitation plate from the lower unit. This was one of the great highlight events for the Willis Comet runabout.

SECOND HEAT

Freddy Goehl

2015

In order to accurately provide a correct history of the Quincy Welding contribution to outboard racing, I asked Paul Christner to provide a short history by one of the family.

The following is his contribution to this book. The article was compiled by Art Neadeck, Gene East and Paul Christner.

Freddy Goehl

SECOND HEAT

Bill Becker

1955

The Alky C Service class and the Evinrude Speedi-twin never had a more dedicated person than Bill Becker, Ohio.

His affection started during the '30's. After the war, he began to work on the motor's lower unit. Whatever the problem, Bill could fix it.

The Speed-twin cigar shaped lower unit originally produced some cavitation problems when elevated to gain speed. Bill was the first to correct that problem.

Bill Becker C-1 Runabout

SECOND HEAT

Tommy Christopher

1970

Mississippi had never been a hot bed for boat racing, but the Christopher family, especially young Tom tried to represent the state. He did – very well!

Prior to becoming an airline pilot, he had an invincible reputation as a first class driver of hot Alky equipment.

Photo - Fox

20 Year Old Tommy Christopher Grenada MS.

SECOND HEAT

Bill Fales & Jerry Peterson

1970

These two loved the big motors. No tiny, slow stuff – just a lot of horsepower.

Bill Fales, left, began his boat racing while living and working in the Long Island Manhattan area. The mafia forced him to move to New Jersey where he became a major factor in making racing fuel. He also found time to head the APA Alky racing division.

Jerry Peterson, Iowa, drove the big D&F class hydro and was constantly up front.

Bob Murphy

1965

Bill Fales & Jerry Peterson

SECOND HEAT

Bob Murphy

Bob Murphy, Springfield, MO purchased Fred Brinkman's Newton C Service motor about 1965 and proceeded to dominate the C Service runabout class for about 10 years.

He was a very successful Illinois plumber and was a popular member of the racing fraternity.

SECOND HEAT

Dick Pond & Billy Seebold

1970

This fax photo is a bit out of focus, however it depicts two giants of boat racing.

Dick Pond is driving Marshall Grant's "Ring of Fire" and Billy Seebold is in "Miss Pam". Pond tended to drive forward in the cockpit with prop shaft out from parallel while using a high rake propeller.

It was typical for each to drive for a sponsor. If one owned top equipment and wanted to win, these two drivers had the ability required.

BT-11 is powered by a Quincy Merc K-4 with a Konig.

Kay Harrison & Papa Smith

Dick Pond & Billy Seebold

SECOND HEAT

Kay Harrison

1960

Kay Harrison had no trouble getting into boat racing. His father, Milford (Millie) was a pioneer – having started in the early days of the sport.

Kay, over the years, probably drove in every Alky hydro class and with success. Millie was the only person in outboard racing who operated the throttle with his right hand and steered with the left.

The Harrisons operated an Ohio machine ship and distributed the Anzani motor after Bill Tenney retired from boat racing.

Photo - Fox

Kay Harrison & Papa Smith

SECOND HEAT

Simison Family

1962

This is a rare photo of all the male Simison family members. From left to right, Jerry, Paul and Dr. Karl Simison, Sr.

In a career of over 20 years, Jerry won hundreds of boat races – National and World Championships. In 1966, he became a member of the Gulf Marine Racing Hall of Fame.

Karl "Jerry" Simison June 1942- February 2014

SECOND HEAT

Mabry Edwards

It was said, in the '30's and '40's that one could throw a rock in any direction, in Florida, and hit water. Doubtless this fact and a salubrious climate, made it became a hotbed of boat racing.

Mabry Edwards was one of a large group of drivers who became famous while headquarted in Florida.

Photo - Fox

Mabry Edwards 1954

SECOND HEAT

1957 McKeesport, PA
NOA National Championship

Champions L to R Kneeling
David Livingston, Bill Tenney, Orlando Torigiani, Tom Small, Doug Creech Jud Davis. L to R Runners Up Standing Henry Taubert, Verg Wheeler, Bill Seebold, Harry Vogts, Steve Gantner, Hap Sharp, P.H. Cornwell, Ralph Dowling, Stanley Levendusky, Clyde Wiseman

SECOND HEAT

R.G. Frawley

About 1970

Dr. Frawley probably had the fastest Alky Evinrude miget motor ever. The motor was tuned by one of the Birbarie clan of New England.

For a period of time in the '50's, the doctor won everything he entered. The rpm of the little 7.5CID motor was a joy to hear by those who knew the antithesis of the Evinrude motor.

Photo - Fox

SECOND HEAT

NOA World Championship
1955
Mt. Carmel, Illinois

Photo – Fox

LtoR David Livingston, Hap Owen, Bill Tenney, Orlando Torigiani
Ellis Willoughby, Dennis Martin, Dorthy Mayer,

SECOND HEAT

Jack Stanford

1960

Jack Stanford, Florida, started boat racing while a young man. He had an attraction for driving a race boat exceeded by few.

He had an engaging personality, everyone liked Jack. His equipment did not always look the best, but it was top class. One knew that he would always be up-front.

Photo - Fox

SECOND HEAT

Pop Willis

Mr. Willis was a formidable competitor. We first saw some of his racing boats in a 1940 boat race at Salton Sea, California. Some Texas driver came to the race with several of his boats. They were competitive, good solid boats of no special performance on the race course.

Several years later, in 1948, at Celina, Tennessee, Bill was astounded at the number of Willis runabouts. We were outnumbered about 10:1. The one pleasing aspect was that sales potential was better than we had anticipated. The Alky division had good sales potential and was worth our concentration.

Again in 1950 at Lake Alfred, Florida it was clear that Willis had the numbers, but he west coast boats had the quality. Sonny King went through the traps at the speed of 56+mph, he was using a very good PR-65. That performance alone told us that we were on solid ground. Unless Willis made a major change, we were on solid ground. Willis probably continued to build racing boats into the '60's but not on a national scale. Their era was over.

My impression of Willis was that racing boats was not critical to them. They probably had other sales interests that were more financially rewarding.

SECOND HEAT

Pop Willis

SECOND HEAT

Judge's Stand

This judge's stand is located next door to the Claude Fox home on the Tennessee River. Thru the '40's, '50's and '60's races were held on this property and one could always go there to test equipment; something that is increasingly hard to find today. Speed and noise factors usually preclude such activity.

Dick O'Dea, Walt Blankenstein, Scott Smith

1970

In the back yard

SECOND HEAT

Dick O'Dea…Patterson, New Jersey

Dick started boat racing in the stock APBA division in 1947 driving an AU runabout. Over the years he drove most every class in outboard racing, hydros and runabouts. He imported the Crescent (Sweden) racing motor for a number of years, till the manufacturer stopped making the motor. Dick became a motor specialist, made a career of putting together specialty motor speed equipment for boat, auto and off-track.

Walt Blankenstein

Walt started working as a high speed motor specialist in the Chicago area. He moved to Lakeland, Florida where, for a short time, he managed Bud Wiget's Magnolia Avenue boat shop but gave that up to move down the street, where he worked on outboard racing motors for the rest of his life.

Scott Smith

Scott imported the Konig racing motor. Scott lived in Dallas, Georgia where he had operated a hardware store. A man of many parts, Scott had been Mayor of Dallas and close relatives owned property in the area. He acquired sole US distributorship of the German Konig motor.

Dick O'Dea, Walt Blankenstine, Scott Smith

SECOND HEAT

Tom Roath

1965

We first ran into Tom Roath in 1969, when we built him a 19' twin engine tunnel boat with which he drove at the two-day marathon on the Colorado River at Havasu City. He was a major boat and motor dealer in Denver at that time. The story of that episode was told in <u>Now & Then</u>.

Prior to all that, Tom had been a prominent Alky boat driver east of Denver. Later in life, he moved down to Florida, got hold of a potent B Konig powered hydro. While testing the equipment with Melvin Cooper at Lake Blacksher, Georgia in 2011, the hydro overturned. Tom was fatally injured.

SECOND HEAT

Addicted to Speed
Captain James McKean

Jim McKean was addicted to excitement. After a career as an all-state basketball player in Iowa, Jim entered the Air Force Academy. He did not like it and had decided to accept a basketball scholarship from Kansas State after his freshman year. A broken foot curtailed his ambition to play basketball. His fate was sealed. Jim was accepted into flight school and sent to Texas, where he met his lovely wife, Tana. This is where Jim was first exposed to racing boats. He had a friend who had an outboard speedboat. Apparently, he ran in local outlaw races. Jim purchased an old runabout with a 20H. He fell in love with racing outboards. Jim had feared that his career as a pilot may lead him to a transport or tanker. He thought this would be boring and he became addicted to speed on the water.

He had no experience flying, unlike the classmates in his flight group. He nearly flunked out except for a special last chance flight test. The instructor told him if he had been required to make one more turn, he would have failed him. Jim was selected for jet training. He became #2 in his class. Only two pilots were selected for fighter jets. #1 selected the new F105 after changing his mind. Jim was to pilot the older, reliable F100. The #1 graduated was sady killed a short time thereafter. If #1 would have chosen the F100, Jim's fate could have been much different. Jim's moniker was "Best of the Best." Even through his commercial career with Continental Airlines. He moved his family to Fountain Valley, CA after leaving the Air Force. He had raced Konigs while in the service in Europe and purchased an old Bellcraft hydro and a very used Konig 500cc. He was not competitive with respect to speed, however, won many races because of his skill and desire. Jim had seen the Konig surfacing lower units. Handicapped by older equipment and his size, Jim thought he could get both to go fast in a straight line. He purchased a Buyers hydro and set numerous APBA and UIM kilo records with this set up. He broke the old records by a large margin due to the special, innovative straightway set up.

Jim had also seen Yamato racing outboards. He became the exclusive distributor for racing engines and imported the first motor, a four pipe 500cc to be run on a Byers in DePue in 1974. The John Ward Trophy race was to be run with the Nationals. The four pipes were stationary. It compared to running today's motors with a pipes fully back all the time. He also ran it on a DeSilva runabout

SECOND HEAT

going about 80mph through the kilos. It came out of the pits going about 75mph. The exhaust system limited to rpm and potential horsepower. Later, a converging two pipe sliding system was developed and he won many championships and set many records. Jim also saw the motors used for stadium racing in Japan. He arranged to purchase the used Model 80 motors for use in the US. They were 20ci and ran as a special "B" class. Later to evolve into many APBA stock and Mod classes as well as the global OSY 400.

SECOND HEAT

This was an NOA event, somewhere in the Midwest about 1958. There appears to be one Anzani powered boat, the rest are Mercury or Konig. Most of the runabouts are DeSilva, two Ashburn (Texas) and on the far right what appears to be a homemade craft.

Photo – Fox

B Runabout

SECOND HEAT

Bill Seebold

A happy Bill Seebold Sr. who has just received the beautiful trophy for winning C Alky Runabout at the 1957 Mt. Carmel, IL NOA National Championship.

Photo - Fox

SECOND HEAT

Harry & Mike O'Brien

1970

Harry O'Brien, Indiana, could easily be defined as one of the giants of outboard racing. His stature as a driver, master mechanic, historian/boat race official is masterful. Son, Mike, carried on as his father's driver and their record of accomplishment is outstanding.

Photo – Fox

Harry O'Brien Pit, Mike O'Brien Driver

SECOND HEAT

Dirk Davison

1971 – Bakersfield, California

Dick Davison started boat racing in the APBA stock program. He owned an air-conditioning business in San Bernadino, CA. Over the years, he parented a large number of boat drivers from within this inland area.

When Lowell Haberman looked for a driver for his Anzani B Runabout he chose Dirk. They put the brand new equipment together at the Lake Mina, for the Bakersfield APBA Nationals. Dirk put together two fine heats and won the Championship.

Haberman was an extremely talented mechanic who mastered all the problems encountered in boat racing. It was often said that Bill Tenney's Anzani was a hard motor to bring to top efficiency. Lowell got all there was from the motor, even Tenney was impressed!

Dick Davison

SECOND HEAT

Dan, Mel & Jerry Kirts

1965

Mel Kirts probably did know he was destined to start on of the iconic family dynasties in boat racing. He drove the big Alky boats. Dan drove everything very well; his career result is perhaps without parallel. Marshal Grant, when asked who had been the best driver of his equipment he replied, "Well, I have had the best, who would be better than Pond or Seebold. But, I have to say that Jerry Kirts was as good. His career in boat racing did not last as long as other members of the family, but he was terrific."

Jack Corner spent a winter in Indiana. One early morning he was going to work when he heard a great noise in a nearby river. Going to the scene, Jack saw that Mel and 3 of his sons had scooped the ice off the water and were testing one of Mel's big hydros.

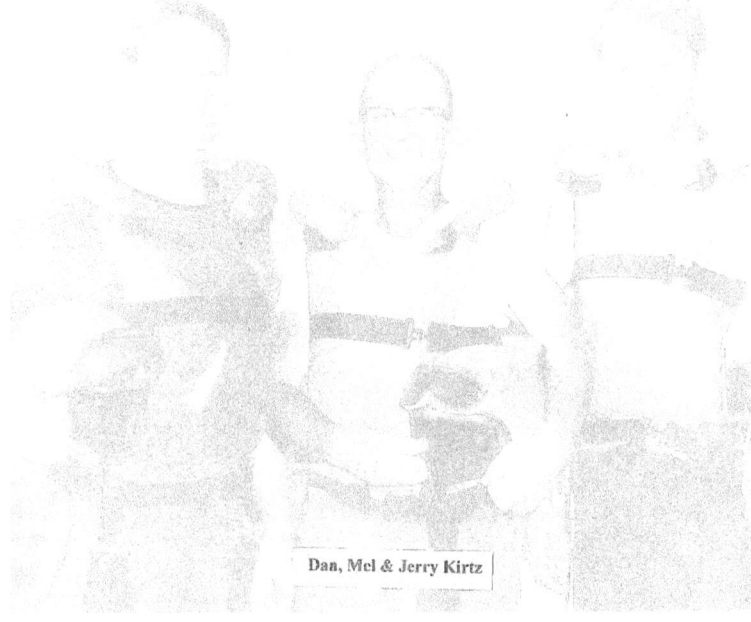

Dan, Mel & Jerry Kirtz

Photo - Fox

Ted Thompson

1965

Ted Thompson

SECOND HEAT

We first ran into Ted Thompson at the APBA Bakersfield, CA Nationals, when he was driving some of Walt Blakenstein's equipment. He was then living in Florida. He started racing with the stock program then phased into the Alky division. He met his wife to be on the trip to California, where they both were looking into the Grand Canyon.

Photo – Fox

Ted Thompson

SECOND HEAT

Eleanor Shakeshaft

193?

Eleanor was one of the better female boat drivers that came along after Evinrude introduced the M class motor in 1933.

Henry, her husband, was well known as a driver in various Alky classes from C Service to F, both runabout and hydro. The family home was originally in the New England area, but sometime in the '30's they moved south to Florida.

Today, their grandchildren are keeping their boat racing tradition alive.

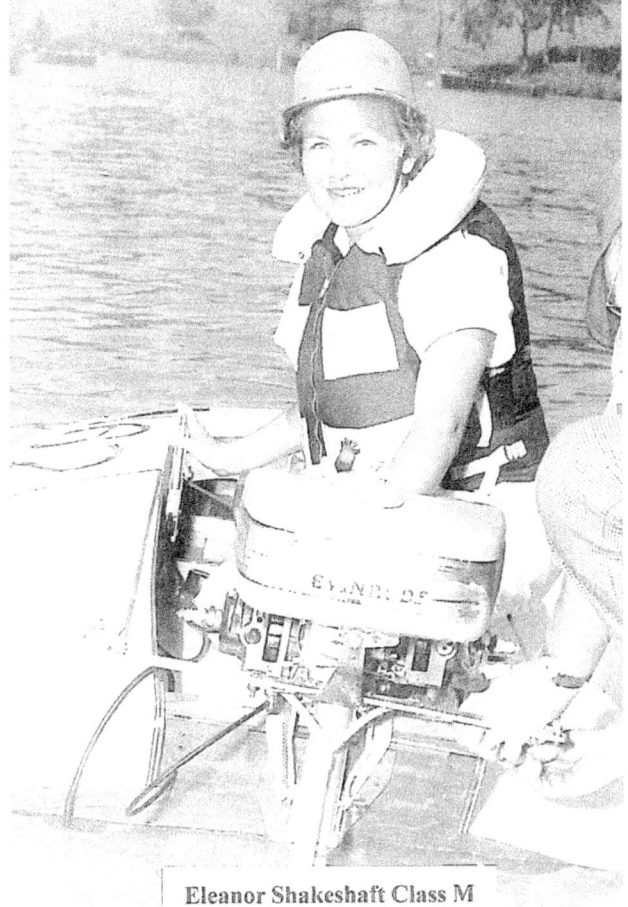

Eleanor Shakeshaft Class M

SECOND HEAT

Harry Brinkman

1972

Harry Brinkman was not really tall, just a bit over 6' but he was a giant in boat racing. His forte was the modified division, mostly soupted-up mercury motors. In fact, he wrote the book ON MERCURY MODIFICATION.

Harry, however, was not one dimensional. He also collected old racing equipment. At one time he purchased a PR-65 from the estate of a good boat racer from the 30's. When the antique category was created by Karl Williams in 1986, Harry put the PR on his 13' chine-turn runabout 99-H and went to the first Antique Nations, De Pere, Wisconsin in 1985. He astounded everyone by winning both boats with the PR.

The feat was remarkable in that he was using a chine-turn runabout (which he flat-turned abound the big 3 buoy course) and a motor and propeller which had not been used for about 15-20 years. The PR, with its 13:19 gear ratio and prop rotation opposite of most other motors, does create a turning problem that a good many drivers find difficulty that they were never able to overcome.

To prove that his win was no fluke, Harry went back to DePere the next year and repeated what had happened the year before. All this against a field of drivers who had raced the PR as a career, had all the technical and good stuff down cold.

His house in Greenwood, Indiana (near the Indy Race Track) was a museum, you had to enter a room sideways!

SECOND HEAT

Harry Brinkman Greenwood IN.

SECOND HEAT

Hershel Starnes

1965

Hershel Starnes did not make his fame as a boat driver, but as a creator of what is generally considered the best of the class C and F Alky lower units.

Evinrude and Johnson lower units used for racing motors did not have after market competition until late in the 30's when other more efficient became available. After WWII, Randolph Hubbel, made a new streamlined unit for the PR and another for the SR "B" motor. Shortly thereafter, Starnes began selling his new creation.

For years, the competition between these two produced more speed and better turning. Each brand had its advocates. The Hubbel B looked more streamlined; the new Starnes looked more bulbous; but Bud Wiget thought it faster.

SECOND HEAT

Wearly Racing Team
2959

Form left to right: Sam, se, John, Sam II, Paul

SECOND HEAT

Dempsey

This is a dog story – no relation to boat racing. But most folks like dogs, so a true story about a remarkable dog should not be amiss.

My cousin Francis and my Aunt Anna owned a 30 acre farm about 7 miles west of Atwater, California. This is in the great San Joaquin Valley, just south of Highway 99. Atwater was just a small village between Merced and Livingston.

The village was too small to have a high school, so one had to travel a further 10 miles to Merced High. Francis often walked all the way, unless someone offered him a ride via a horse or wagon, or the rate truck or auto.

On or about his 10th birthday, Francis received a German Sheppard puppy, who received the name of Dempsey. Jack would have been proud! Dempsey soon proved to be a family member of great importance. No one gave him any formal training. He acquired his abilities and knowledge through observation and intelligence.

In the 20's and 30's, a newspaper was more than a thing in which to start a fire. It was perhaps the only practical source one had for general news and gossip.

Because the San Joaquin Valley was not yet on the national power grid, radio was not available. Great circulation magazines like the Saturday Evening Post and Colliers were not readily available.

Therefore, the evening local newspaper was a thing of importance. It was read thoroughly. Even the obituaries!

The routine never varied. Francis and Dempsey walked, ran or skipped to the mailbox at 5:30 every day for the paper. The mailbox was about 2 miles from the farm, out on Highway 99.

Dempsey grew to full size. He learned to herd the chickens when Anna called to feed them by spreading various feed. He protected the vegetable garden from rabbits and birds. He would not let the geese wander off the ranch. It would be proper to say that he was in command of the farm animals. He maintained order, in a gentle, firm manner.

One day Francis, for some reason or another was not able to go after the paper. No one gave the paper any thought. The folks were gathered under the grape arbor, about dusk when Dempsey same trotting up with the paper between his teeth.

SECOND HEAT

Everyone was shocked. There had been no thought of the paper. Yet, here was Dempsey with the paper!

Dempsey dropped the paper in front of Mace, Anna's husband.

After the shock, Dempsey received plenty of food, praise, petting and affection. The family did not know to make the errand a continuing thing. They need not have worried. Dempsey, for the rest of his life, continued to pick up the evening paper. It was his contribution to the family that treasured him as a true member of the family.

Don't ask.

SECOND HEAT

Louis Williams

1975

We really appreciated Louis (Fillinger) Williams. He made us look good! For many years he drove an Ashburn runabout and constantly ran in the middle of the pack at the usual big race.

Despite the friendly controversial chit-chat no one ever doubted that Louis was on extremely talented driver.

Louis Williams

We sold him a boat in 1978, with which he won the APBA class A (250 CID) Runabout Championship at Acworth, Georgia in 1980.

Louis Williams was a mortician. He generously offered to take care of us when we were ready to leave life! He and team member, Joe Rome, made their home in Texas.

Photo – Fox

SECOND HEAT

Ellis Willoughby

1953

We first sold a 13' Alky runabout to Ellis in 1953. In 1958, he beat all the competition at Mt. Carmel, IL. NOA, C Runabout Alky class, with his PR motor.

At that time the Johnson PR was beginning to get serious competition from the Quincey Merc and Konig was about to enter the American market with other motors than the evident class A, 15 CID motor. Although the Willoughby performance was not the last, it was certainly the ultimate performance of that grand piece of machinery.

Three years later at the same place, in the same manner, Bill Seebold, Sr, repeated this performance with the PR. I don't remember the PR Johnson winning another championship until the antique program was created in 1986.

Ellis Willoughby

SECOND HEAT

Wayne Baldwin

They say everything in Texas is big. Wayne Baldwin was perhaps typical. His hometown was Alice, Texas and he liked big power race boats. He drove C, D &F hydros.

He began using the Butt's Aerowing hydro and became the man to beat. He and his father traveled the US and Europe for the joy of competition and test themselves with the best on hand. To list Wayne's record of accomplishments would not really indicate their contribution to boat racing.

Photo - Fox

Wayne Baldwin

SECOND HEAT

Bill Tenney
1960

Bill Tenney married shortly before the 1958 NOA Nationals at McAlester, Oklahoma. In the photo above, son, David appears to be about 1 ½ to 2 years old, which would place the above location in Springfield, Illinois – the 1959 NOA Nationals.

Tenney stopped driving about this time. He continued to import the Anzani racing motor – until the Harrison family, Ohio, purchased the franchise.

A short time later, we heard that Bill had made a deal with the Scott McCulloch Company to establish a new outboard speed record, to wrest that crown then held by OMC Entrop Team.

It would be interesting to know who had overall control of the effort – who provided the money and importantly, who made the important decisions.

What Johnny Parson, of Indianapolis fame and Dan Foster, unlimited hydroplane; had to do with the project, is unknown, except that their reputations could or would be valuable should the endeavor succeed. Both were rumored to have been involved. Perhaps one would have been the driver!

We were to learn that this grand attempt failed. The di Priolo lower unit failed soon after testing began. Rumor says that the outfit got up to about 80mph before the failure.

Scott McCulloch pulled the plug on the project. They must have been disappointed. The company had tried to participate in various boat racing activities without much success.

The McCulloch Company gradually eased out of outboard motors, their chainsaw operation had became a development firm which developed Site Six on the Colorado River (Arizona side) which turned into the thriving town now called Havasu City.

SECOND HEAT

TALKING IT OVER......LEFT, JOHNNY PARSONS, FAMOUS INDIANAPOLIS 500 MILE SPEED PILOT DISCUSSES THE FLYING SCOTT WITH DANNY FOSTER. FOSTER, INTERNATIONALLY KNOWN SPEED PILOT ATTEMPTING TO BE THE FIRST DRIVER IN THIS COUNTRY TO PILOT AN OUTBOARD BOAT OVER 100 MILES PER HOUR.

SECOND HEAT

This photo is a good view of the di Priolo lower unit. Two 60Hp Scott powerheads were mated together into a gear box, then attached to the 3 foot long lower unit.

SECOND HEAT

Bill Tenney & David

Though one cannot be certain, the driver does not seen to be Bill Tenney. The boat is headed toward California from a location on the Colorado River, Arizona side, north of Parker about 30-40 miles.

SECOND HEAT

SECOND HEAT

Though one cannot be certain, the driver does not seen to be Bill Tenney. The boat is headed toward California from a location on the Colorado River, Arizona side, north of Parker about 30-40 miles.

SECOND HEAT

Congress & Laurel

1933

We were living in Pacific Grove, in a duplex on the corner of Congress and Laurel. I remember that because my mother made Bill and me place the location firmly in mind case of emergency.

One day, I was near the garage when a passing older man stopped at a pile of wood lying about and said, "Young man, do you know what that wood is? It's a rare and beautiful wood – Mahogany." I replied, "Yes, my father builds boats out of it. We burn this scrap in the fireplace."

The pile consisted of mostly 5/16" planking from 6" to 8" wide. It was used for bottom planking and sides. There were some odd size material mostly milled stock. My father purchased this Philippine mahogany from big lumber companies in San Francisco and Oakland. Price of mahogany, at that time, was about $.07-$.08 per foot, milled. At that price, one could burn the scrap.

The old man shook his head and walked away.

SECOND HEAT

THE FOLLOWING ARTICLE WAS GIVEN TO RALPH DONALD BY JULIE FOX – AUTHOR UNKNOWN

W. CLAUDE FOX

Parents: H.M. and Dinah Fox
Father – farmer, owner of a country store and grist mill
Place of Birth: Andersonville, TN
Schooling: Belmont Grammar;
Andersonville High School, Class of 1927;
Attended Knoxville Business College and the University of Tennessee
Spouse: Julie Boykin Fox, married, 1970

W. Claude Fox has shaped his life around a love of the water. He has been called "Dean of the Waterways" by virtue of the sheer magnitude of his involvement with all aspects of boating, from sales to safety, but especially racing. According to a prominent writer for boating publications and one of Fox's peers, "…there has never been a single individual who has done more for power boating in general and boat racing in particular with W. Claude Fox."

The desire to advance his favorite sport, which Fox calls "the greatest spectacle of all competition racing in all sports," led to charter memberships and official positions within countless boating organizations, most notably the National Outboard Association, where he served as executive director for over 30 years.

During the past 60 years, Fox has accumulated an astonishing number of awards and trophies, many of them from the United States Coast Guard. He is one of the first members of the U.S. Coast Guard Auxiliary in the nation and has the longest service record of any living member. Fox helped form one of the first Flotillas in the Auxiliary, 12-1, Division 12, in Knoxville, and is the only surviving charter member of the Flotilla. He has received over 29 awards from the Coast Guard, including two of the highest given.

SECOND HEAT

Fox did not win his reputation only through activities with the Auxiliary. He began his boating career as a race driver but eventually became one of the most influential and respected officials in the sport. He is skilled organizer with a no-nonsense approach to getting the job done.

Looking at Fox, it is difficult to believe that this tall, still slender man, a good many years past retirement, has been a part of the boating world for so long. He is a modest man of innate courtesy who readily admits he is a lot older than he looks. But he is cagey about revealing this age – not because of vanity, he says, but because he is tired of not being believed. The only problem his doctors can find when he goes in for his check-up is a hearing loss he attributes to the loudness of early racing boats.

He is frequently asked to resume leadership of various boating organizations, which he always declines. However, he plans to continue his work with the Coast Guard and frequently donates his time for charitable activities.

BACKGROUND

Fox was born the son of a farmer, H.M fox, in Andersonville, deep in the heart of landlocked Tennessee. One of five children, he helped with the farm and the general store his father also owned, selling everything from grain and feed to caskets. He didn't start school until he was eight and never did get in the habit of eating breakfast. Later, when he was in the Army and still not eating breakfast, he received a 25 cent refund for every morning meal he missed!

After graduating from Andersonville High School in 1927, Fox enrolled in Knoxville Business College.

BOATING: THE EARLY YEARS

Almost as soon as he arrived in Knoxville, Fox discovered the pleasures of boating. He remembers putting in for the first time under the Gay Street Bridge and spending every chance he got on the water. Boating was more of a challenge then than it is today, with unreliable wood boats and motors. Fox says the trick was always to head out upstream, so you could return by floating downstream if your engine conked out. "It was a rare thing back then to complete even a short trip without engine problems." He recalls.

SECOND HEAT

Fox bought his first boat by accident. A man named Lawson Oglesby owned a dock on the downtown waterfront at the foot of Market Street, where a half dozen boats were docked. Fort Loudoun Lake had not yet been impounded and the river's current was swift, making it tricky to dock a boat.

"I was hanging out down at the dock one day," fox remembers, "when a boatman who kept a boat there came down the river and took a shot at the dock and missed it. He tried to turn around and come back upstream, but something happened and he was in the river. Since he couldn't swim, he darn near drowned before we could get him out. When he finally got on dry land, he announced that his boat was for sale because he didn't ever intend to go on the water again as long as he lived." Fox took the boat off his hands for $150. The incident must have made a lasting impression on him because he became a fervent advocate of boating safety.

He and his friends began racing their boats, even before manufacturers were building many racing boats and motors. "You just got out and raced with what you had," he said. One of their favorite runs was along the Tennessee River before Fort Loudoun Dam was built. Much of the time was spent lifting boats over the rocks, and propellers were regularly chewed up on the shoals, but none of the quelled their enthusiasm for the sport.

The impoundment of Norris Lake in 1936 changed the face of boating in Knoxville. The lake provided less strenuous boating than the waters of the Tennessee River and interest in boating took off. Fox remembers that "there would be hundreds of people at the shore wanting to ride up the lake with me and a buddy of mine. We knew it was against the law to charge them for riding, but people would still throw a few quarters our way. Of course, a quarter was worth a lot back then."

As the lake began to fill with novice boaters, someone was always having a breakdown and Fox was usually there to help them out since he spent every spare moment on the water. A friend finally suggested to Fox that he ought to go into boat sales, and he says the notion "really rang a bell," since, as a dealer he could charge for many of the services he rendered for free, and he could make his living doing what he loved best – working with boats.

In 1938 he opened a marine dealership in Knoxville, Marine Sales Company, at 1701 North Broadway, with the aid of John Cox of the Bank of Knoxville. As the first marine dealer in Knoxville, he sold the first Mercury motors built by the company, as well as Martin motors and Gray marine

SECOND HEAT

motors. His inventory included boats built by Sea Ray, Century, Gar Wood, Glaspar, and Crosby, and cruisers built by Owens, Matthews, and Richardson.

Fox, who always believed that what was good for boat racing was good for business, cultivated a close working relationship with the media. He probably was one of the pioneers of media events, traveling to a boat racing site a day or two early in order to hold a press conference. Since sitting back and waiting for someone else to get the job done was not his style, he pursued the media connection by becoming a founding member of two publications, *Tennessee Outdoor Writers Association* and *Southeastern Outdoor Press Association*, with whom he has a lifetime membership. He also founded one of boat racing's most popular magazines, *Rooster Tail*, which became the official publication of the National Outboard Association. He served as editor and photographer, beginning one of the largest collections of boat racing photographs in the nation.

Photo - Fox

One of the early sales was to Bruce Keener, the president of C.M. McClung and Co., one of the largest wholesale hardware companies in Knoxville. Keener, his wife and twelve-year-old son, were present for the lesson in docking the boat. Keener was so nervous he couldn't land the 26-foot Richardson cabin cruiser after a number of attempts, Finally, the son asked permission to try. "To my disbelief, he bought the cruiser to dock perfectly!" Fox remembers.

Fox lost contact with the young man until 1989, when he received a letter from retired rear admiral, Bruce Keener III. In the letter, Keener remembers that early initiation into the art of docking a boat with Fox as teacher. 'from that beginning, I continued my association with the water in a Navy career that spanned 38 ½ years…and I am proud to say that ship handling was one of my conspicuous strengths throughout my career," Keener wrote. Fox, a long-time member of the Coast Guard, enjoys saying that the Coast Guard taught the Navy how to pilot a boat.

SECOND HEAT

About the same time, for both business and pleasure, he began organizing boat clubs, some of which are still active today. He was the founder, a charter member and request commodore of the oldest boat club in the state of Tennessee, the Knoxville Racing club. The club later changed its name to the Knoxville Boat Club and awarded Fox a lifetime membership. He is a charter member of the Dixie Motor Boat Association, and served as commodore until 1943. He also helped found the Knoxville Yacht Club, now the Fort Loudon Yacht Club.

BUSINESS ASSOCIATIONS

As a marine dealer in the late thirties, Fox carried products of some of the most famous names in boat manufacturing. One manufacturer he remembers most fondly is Gar Wood. Wood, the inventor of the dump truck and a well-known race driver, was the first to drive a boat at 100 miles per hour. He manufactured elegant wood-sided boats, much prized by collectors today. Fox met Wood during a trip the latter made before the war to see the Tennessee waterways. The two became friends and Wood offered to customize a boat for Fox.

Fox specialized two modifications to a 19 foot, double cockpit forward runabout. The first was the addition of an engine taken from one of his racing boats, to which the factory agreed. The second modifications was the addition of a walkway between the two forward cockpits. This is where he ran into trouble with Wood, who felt the change of design would weaken the boat. But Fox's wishes prevailed, and he speaks with unmistakable fondness of the lovely mahogany-decked, white-sided runabout that roared over the waters of the lake with its thunderous racing engine at the unheard of speed of 61 m.p.h.

Fox used the boat until he reported to the Army, at which time he sold it for $800 to a local doctor. It sat unused for years and then was sold several times. It finally ended up in Massachusetts in the hands of a member of the Gar Wood Club, whose members devoted to restoring Gar Wood boats to their former glory. The gentleman contacted the president of the club and the modifications to his boat and was put in touch with Fox. He also noticed an indentation on the dash and Fox explained that he had removed the silver plate put there by wood which stated the boat had been especially built for Commodore W. Claude Fox.

SECOND HEAT

"The gentleman wanted the plate badly," Fox says, "and for a long time I refused. But the last time he called, I told him if he would bring the boat to Knoxville and let me take a picture of it, I'd give him the plate."

In addition to Gar Wood, Fox enjoyed what he calls "splendid relationships" with all marine supply company officials. Another relationship he vividly remembers was with a man which he describes as "my friend, my enemy, my friend, my enemy, and my friend, in that order. This individual thought he had to be first – and usually was – in everything. There was never another one and will not be another like him. It would take hours for me to relate all my contacts and events that came my way by this man. If it was not him in person, there were telephone calls or telegrams and letters from his employees, company officers or attorneys.

"I'm sure anyone in the past or present connected with boats will know I am referring to a man I am proud to have known, the one and only Carl Kiekhaefer. I will cite one event – the setting was a 2-day racing event in Kentucky. There was a rule in the racing organization that would not permit new engines to be introduced during the racing season. This man sends two of his company men to persuade me to permit the engine in question to enter not only this race but others in the future. I was confronted all day and night at meetings called by these two who were constantly in touch with Carl.

"To make a long story short, the second morning of the event one of the men said Carl told them not to leave the state until I approved their request. My answer to them was 'you'd better start now to locate a place of abode in the great state of Kentucky!'"

THE OFFICIAL FOX

Being a business man didn't keep Fox from racing boats at every opportunity. He loved racing on area waters, which he feels produce the best race courses in the nation, and can remember there being a boat race almost every weekend during the summer months. The years spent as a race driver firmly bonded him with the other drivers, and in later years he would be one of their strongest advocates as an official, never favoring them, but making sure they got what they deserved.

As the time, Jim Mulroy of Chicago headed up the pre-war National Outboard Association (NOA), the outboard racing sanctioning group. He suggested Fox become an official, telling him he was a good driver, but he'd be an even better official. Fox loved driving, but agreed. It was a decision that suited him well, and he became one of the sport's most respected officials.

SECOND HEAT

World War II put an end to the NOA and boat racing. After the war, the American Power Boat Association became the only body controlling boat racing. Fox worked as an official with them for several years, serving on the board the same year as Guy Lombardo. However, this group was not as popular with the drivers as the former NOA, and Fox, known as a race driver's official, was approached frequently by drivers to reactivate the NOA. When the motor manufacturing sponsor of APBA got wind of the plan, that sponsor offered Fox the presidency of APBA to keep him from reactivating NOA. "That was the wrong thing to say to me," Fox says emphatically. "I didn't believe in any manufacturer controlling the associations."

Finally, in 1951, Fox agreed to get the new NOA off the ground and moved the headquarters to Knoxville so he could continue with his marine sales business. His intent was to guide the helm only temporarily, but he held the unpaid position of executive director until the NOA closed its doors in the mid-eighties, primarily due to insurance costs. Fox says he still received frequent calls to reactivate the organization, but always declines.

His favorite memory during his years as an official is the time he met President Franklin D. Roosevelt. Fox was in Chattanooga to referee a boat race that was part of the dedication ceremonies for the newly built Chicamauga Dam. He also helped oversee the construction of the platform for officials, in particular the ramp to be use for President Roosevelt, who was confined to a wheelchair. He became good friends with the Secret Service men accompanying the President, and it was one of the agents who called Fox over to meet the President as he sat in his car.

"After over 50 years as an official," he reflects, "I think the time is possibly overdue for me to get back in the trenches of boat racing. I not only was a race official, but I was at all times looking for good race sites and good sponsors. I searched out many places where boat races were never expected to take place. Many times, a first-time racing event took place in one of these places and continued annually for 25-30 years.

"I have seen some of the largest entry fields of drivers in the history of boat racing. I recall one in Illinois, not a well-known event, that drew 572 entries. For various reasons, I will never forget the field of drivers that entered the race in Chattanooga, TN, where President Franklin Roosevelt dedicated the Chicamauga Dam: Class A hydroplane, 42 entries; Class B hydroplane, 45 entries; Class C hydroplane, 39 entries. Jim Mulroy instructed me to start all classes with this enormous entry list. There were nine Class C hydros spilled in the first turn – two of the nine were Fred Jacoby and

SECOND HEAT

Dick Neal, the two most famous hydroplane builders. I might add that I refereed many races where Neal and Jacoby entered, and I doubt if there were many races in which they were entered that one or both didn't jump the gun.

"It has been said that I refereed more races than anyone in the nation, and for sure I am convinced that either as an official or head of the racing association, I have been connected with more boats races than any other individual in the nation.

"I will always have a spot in my heart for the hundreds of drivers who made me look good to the races sponsors by coming by the hundreds to the many races that I sold to the sponsors. They never let me down. It makes my day anytime I come in contact with them, the best friends I ever had."

WORLD WAR II

What the Depression couldn't do, the Second World War did: it got Fox out of marine sales. He sold his business in 1941 and spent the next four years as an officer with the Army Corps of engineers Amphibious Command. He remembers receiving a call from Washington D.C. from the Army's Corp of Engineers. Boating manufacturer Gar Wood has recommended Fox to the Corp, which was developing an Amphibious command and was in need of men with extensive boating experience. The Army offered Fox a commission as second lieutenant and the chance to be a part of forming the Amphibious Engineers.

Knowing he was going to be drafted anyway, Fox accepted the offer and served as head of the maintenance regiment. He participated in over 25 landings in the New Guinea area, ending up in the Philippines. He remembers landing on the same beach as General MacArthur on his (Fox's) birthday October 20, 1944. He was sent to Borneo to work with the Australians for an amphibious landing, later returning to the Philippines to train for the landing in Japan, something, he feels in retrospect, would have been suicidal. The atomic bomb saved him from that particular fate and he left the service at the rank of Captain, decorated with the Purple Heart and the Bronze Star.

Fox remembers he almost didn't get out of the Army. General W.F. Heavey was intent on keeping him in the amphibious division after the war, and repeatedly offered Fox a promotion and extended furlough to entice him to stay, offers Fox always refused. In a last ditch effort to hang on to Fox, the general sent orders for his transfer when Fox arrived to claim his discharge papers. Because he had accumulated enough points for discharge, he was able to refuse the transfer. He chuckles when he

SECOND HEAT

remembers one of the General's aides saying that Fox was the only man he knew who turned down the General and got away with it. He still has a letter he received from general Heavey in which Heavey personally thanked him for his "fine work" during the War.

AFTER THE WAR

When Fox returned to Knoxville in 1946, he wasted no time starting another marine sales business. Along with Ben Bower, he founded the firm Bowfox at 110 E. Vine. He later bought out Bower's share of the business and changed the name to Fox and Company, moving the store to 1024 N. Broadway.

For the next 19 years, he remained active as the executive director of the NOA. He also organized the first boat show in Knoxville, the Tennessee Valley Sport Show, now known as the Greater Knoxville Sportsman Show. He also organized the Knoxville Boat Show. In 1965, he sold Fox and Company to Jim Whaley when he retired.

Because he was retired from marine sales didn't mean Fox was idle. In 1952 he was appointed marine surveyor by Govenor Gordon Browning and organized a survey company, Seafox and Associates, after he retired as a racing official. He operated the company until the late eighties. He also remained active with the Coast Guard Auxiliary in the area of boating safety, conducting record numbers of Courtesy Motorboat Exams.

During the early years of boat racing, Fox became interested in photography. He started shooting his own pictures of the races because he was dissatisfied with the quality of boating pictures being taken at the time. His hobby nearly became a full-time enterprise, and he estimates that he has the largest collection of boat racing pictures, slides and negatives – between 7 and 10,000 – in the country. His photographs, some of which have become famous, appeared regularly in numerous magazines and Coast Guard newsletters. He is the official photographer for the Auxiliary and for years was the official photographer for the NOA. He owns three cameras, and for a while had his own dark room. He recently sold the dark room. He recently sold the darkroom equipment, saying it was a lonely place, but kept three cameras that he uses constantly, photographing civic events. He was the official photographer for the Knoxville Bicentennial Celebration and continues his association with the Dogwood Arts Festival as official photographer.

In the late eighties, Fox founded yet another organization, this one close to his heart. The Pioneer Outboard Drivers Association is made up of the drivers from the early years of boat racing – the old-

SECOND HEAT

timers, as Fox calls them, who helped keep racing alive during a time when manufacturers weren't' interested in making racing parts, and drivers had to be backyard mechanics. The organization exists to bring the drivers together once a year for a reunion. Fox says this event is "the outstanding event of my life. As an official, I couldn't be too friendly with the drivers. Now we can hobnob – it makes my year every time I have the opportunity to meet with these guys who are the best friends I ever had on earth. The last driver against which I competed, Chuck Hogle, passed away a few years ago.

"Boat racing was and is my favorite sport. I will continue my love for the sport and live hoping that it will reach the pinnacle of my dreams, that it will be put in its rightful place, as it is the most exciting of all racing sports. Remember, in the past, boat racing was far more popular than car racing. The Indy 500 was about the only popular car event in the nation. It is well where car racing stands today. How did it get there?

"I am often asked my views of what it would take to put the sport where it belongs. My reply would not set well with many people. I recently promised myself at this stage of my life to refrain from giving my views.

"I am not saying I have all the answers to today's way of boat racing. My way, in retrospect, worked in my day. I always held out that the drivers were the stars of the show, not me or any of my officials. I can truthfully say, as a referee and executive director, I had far more problems with officials that I did with drivers.

"I remember one race in south Alabama. I drove down and took a starter with me. During the race he wasn't handling the flags the way he was supposed to. After the first race, I called his hand (corrected him). When he did it the second time, I called him again. So he told me I could just start the race myself. I told him to give me the flags and as he handed them to me I said he could catch the next bus back home. I was about to the start the race and he comes walking back, with a big smile on his face. He took the flag and started the race correctly. It was the bus that did it. He didn't want to lose his free ride with me!

Today Fox lives on his riverfront home next door to the boat club he helped found, surrounded by the water he loves. His plans for the future include "wearing out my three cameras" taking photographs for his friends and civic organizations, and continuing his association with Auxiliary's boat safety program. He looks forward to his volunteer work and giving something back to the community, he says.

SECOND HEAT

"I will continue, as long as I am physically able, to lend my services to my many community projects," Fox explains. "For years I have been interested in raising money for various civic organizations with boat racing and other ways. Among my trophies I have received is a beautiful plaque from the Sertoma Club with the inscription, 'For Aiding the Club to raise $50.000.'

When the time comes, Fox has made arrangements to be cremated and have his ashes scattered on the waters in front of his home. Until then, he enjoys sharing each day with the most important person in his life, his wife, Julie. He notes that Julie's love of the water and boats surpasses even his own – although one might have a hard time believing anyone is more devoted to boating than Fox. Their mutual passion for boating, he feels, has been an important ingredient to the continued success of their marriage.

"I will always enjoy my boats. I have kept a fleet of three pleasure boats for years. After Julie and I ceased water skiing, I decided to sell one, which cut my fleet to two boats. After several months, we got the urge to have a boat with runabout speed and I purchased one of the small Jet Boats, so now I am back to three boats. The runabout carries the name I have used for years with my racing boats. The Jet boat is imp 27, meaning that in my many years of boating, I have owned 27 racing and pleasure boats. Some would say I love boating, and I will agree, adding that I do love boating, possibly more that I should!

But Fox will never say that about his life's companion.

"To all my good health, all my present activities, I have to give full credit to my lovely wife, Julie," he says fondly. "She daily aids me to perform all my current activities. I informed her on our 25th wedding anniversary that I live her more, <u>much more</u>, than I did 25 years ago."

W. CLAUDE FOX

1927: Bought first boat, an outboard hydroplane, from Roy Evans for $150

1936: *Charter member, Knoxville Racing Club, lifetime membership, later changed to Knoxville Boat Club

*Charter Member, Knoxville Boat Club (oldest in the state, with a race course on which more records were set than any other in the country)

*Charter Member, Dixie Motor Boat Association – southeast commander until 1943

SECOND HEAT

*Charter Member, Knoxville Yacht Club, now Fort Loudon Yacht Club

1938: Opened first marine dealership in Knoxville, Marine Sales Company, 1701 N. Broadway; sold in 1941

1939: *Helped found US Coast Guard Reserve, Flotilla 12-1 in Knoxville; only surviving member of founding group; longest service in the nation
*First boat on Norris Lake; also first boating accident and citation

1941: Joined the Army Corp of Engineers as a Second Lieutenant with newly formed Amphibious command; Served in Australia, New Guinea and Philippines; Discharged as a Captain with the Purple Heart and the Bronze Star in 1945

1946: Opened Bowfox marine dealership, 110 E. Vine, with Ben Bower; later bought out Bower, reopening as Fox and Co., 1024 N. Broadway.

1951: Named Executive Director of the National Outboard Association, held position until the mid eighties

1965: Sold Fox and Co to Jim Whaley

1970: Married Julie Boykin

1989: Celebrated 50 years with the Coast Guard Auxiliary

SECOND HEAT

Lightle Samsel

Middle '50's

Samsel bought one of Tom Newton's C Service Evinrude motors – one of the first to get a hold of one of the most dominant motors' in outboard racing history.

At one time or another, Samsel held all the records possible for C Service hydro.

Lightle Samsel Electric City Washington

SECOND HEAT

C.A Buddy Smith

1965

Buddy Smith was a Floridian. And in his era, Florida was a mecca for boat racing. The Florida winter grapefruit circuit was famous all over the world. At one time or another, it was common for European boat race drivers to winter in Florida and participate through the winter months.

Smith made his living by working for some of the big boat manufacturing companies in the area. His expertise was that of a mold maker. He designed and built is own hydroplanes.

At one time he had a problem with one of his creations. It had a flaw in that he kept going over backwards. It was fast, but had that tendency to flip. He got other drivers to drive the boat, they all said the same thing, the boat was OK, no flip problem.

Buddy's driving style was not to kneel down deep in the cockpit, but to remain a good bit upright. It was evident that the wind force on his chest, at speed, was enough to blow the boat over! Lesson learned.

C.A.Buddy Smith

SECOND HEAT

Lee St. Clair

1961

A dedicated boat race driver. No one was a more enthusiastic participant than St. Clair. It did not matter that he was not a front runner, he was involved and that was what mattered.

Photo - Fox

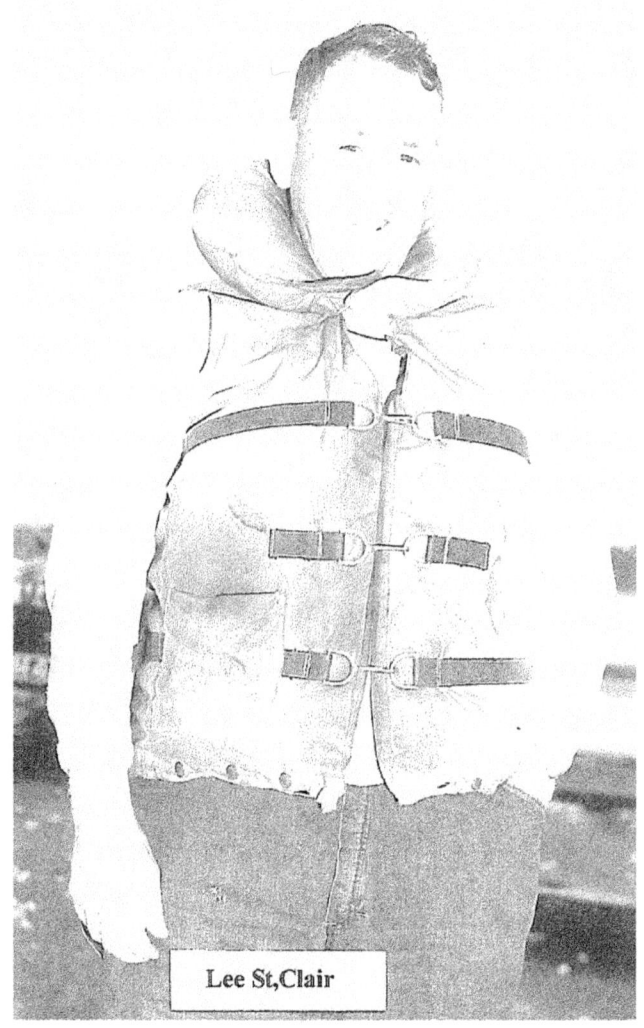

SECOND HEAT

Walter Courtois & Bob Lowrey

circa 1960

Two prominent mid-west drivers of 1950 & 1960 Alky and Modified equipment. Courtois bought a number of our boats. He was known as an up-front aggressive driver.

Bob Lowrey may have lived in the St. Louis, MO area and raced mostly with Mercury power.

Photo - Fox

Left Walter Courtois & Right Bob Lowrey

SECOND HEAT

George Mishey

1955

George Mishey started boat racing in Ohio. He moved to Phoenix after WWII.

His forte was class F and the 4-60 Evinrude racing motor. He was good and he began building a competitive line of outboard hydros.

He went to Celina, Tennessee in 1948. He either forgot or did not know that the area was county dry. After spending a night in jail, George resumed his boat racing activities. No problem, life is good!

Photo - Fox

Pappy George Mishey Phoenix AZ.

SECOND HEAT

Casablanca

It may not be your favorite movie. Bogart is not my favorite actor. However, at the time, I was in love with Ingrid Bergman.

It is probably regrettable that Barry Fitzgerald and John Wayne were not part of the cast. Maybe not; can one see Wayne as the long suffering, understanding dolt of a husband or singing the Marsellaise in front of the orchestra?

Despite that, Casablanca is, if not the first, up alongside whatever is my all-time movie. It is hard perhaps, to pin-point why this may be so. There is not a lot of action, no one tears up the furniture, it's mostly dialogue and it makes it a great picture.

The movie was made in 1943. I was stationed in St. Cloud, a Paris suburb. It is on the southwest side, across the Seine River. We could take the metro train into Paris every night because American army personnel could ride free. There were no taxicabs operating, no gas for civilian's use (that is another story).

Most of us considered the heart of Paris to be on the right bank, on the Champs Elysees between the Arc de Triomphe and the Place de la Concorde. The roadway is about 200 yards wide and stretches about 2 miles between the two monuments.

The American Army had leased all the movie theatres along the Boulevard. One was showing the movie Casablanca.

One early December 1944 evening, I was strolling the Champs and decided to look at Casablanca. I was not much interested in North Africa. It had been liberated by the Allies and it wasn't Italy. What could be exciting about Casablanca?

However, Ingrid Bergman was part of the show and I loved her. Betty Grable was not even a close second! Bogart was OK. Not in the same league as John Wayne, but OK.

The movie was an experience, a classic. It had everything; drama, conflict, suspense, surprise, iconic song and soundtrack and dialogue that even now is part of our general conversation. The folks who put on the movie together probably did not know they had created one for the ages, it was not really big budget, except perhaps for the cast.

SECOND HEAT

A guess is that Casablanca did not require Cecil B. DeMille background. No need the cast, the music, dialogue, the story makes Casablanca what it is – an all-time classic. It may not be on your top ten list but think about it.

- Who could have played the piano and sung "As Time Goes By" better than D. Wilson
- What better place to put the Vichy/Travel Pass than in the piano
- How amazing that the ball rested on 17 twice
- How satisfactorily that Major Strasser gets his in the end
- Even Ingrid is surprised when she and her husband fly off in the end
- Rick and the Colonel walk off into the night (I wonder what became of them?)
- "Here's to you, kid"
- As Time Goes By – the song
- "As honest as the day is long"
- "I was well paid"
- "play the Marsellaise!"
- "go back to Serbia"
- "be careful when you get to Brooklyn"
- "play it again, Sam"
- "I'm shocked, shocked, that there's gambling going on here!"
- "How long will our money last?"
- "shoot me, I'm dead anyway"
- "why did she come to my joint"
- "she is a new second front, all by herself"
- "sounds like they're about 20 miles away"
- "let's get married on the train"

SECOND HEAT

When I sat down in the theatre, a GI next to me said, "would you like an apple?" and handed me a red delicious apple. It proved to be hard, firm and crisp, almost as if it had been picked off the Washington State tree a few days prior. If there had been any question as to which side would win WWII, this simple example of a fresh apple from western America shipped to France for GI consumption should have supplied the answer.

SECOND HEAT

100 Miles = 10 Gallon's Gas + 1 Qt Oil

The big Outboard race in 1947 was to be held in Texas at a site in Brownwood. This is a tale of three Californians who made the trip. The adventure is told by Orville Brisbin, who related the journey to us in 1977.

Orville from Napa, CA, had started boat racing in 1931 by buying a Johnson KR motor and a conventional hydro from my father. He was probably about 50 years old at the time. In 1933, he won the first leg of the Hearst Memorial Perpetual Trophy, the second in 1935 and then he retired the trophy in 1937. All these performances against the best competition in the western US. The Hearst Regatta was supported and sponsored by the Hearst newspaper chain.

During WWII, Orville was too old for armed forces service, so he worked at the Mare Island Navy Yard. He had enlisted in 1917 and had served in France. His service in France had been eventful. Most young men at that time did not know how to drive a vehicle. Orville knew all about both auto and trucks because his father was a general contractor who used such machinery on an "everyday" basis.

When the brass learned that he was an experienced driver/mechanic they put him to work as a chauffeur of "very important" brass. He saw most of Western Europe and he did not want to go back.

Onto Brownwood, TX...

The phone call was from Harold Ashley. He was going to the APBA Nationals and wanted him to go along. Jack Dempsey had agreed to come along.

Ashley was a well known outboard race boat driver who lived in Marysville. He had campaigned both hydro and runabout very successfully prior to WWII. On this trip he was to take only his F hydro. One rig to keep the boat light and make it easy for his Old's to pull.

"I was not doing anything important at the time and thought that a trip to Texas would be interesting. Ashley seemed to be a reasonable person. Dempsey may be a problem, not serious, but a bit odd. He had been around boat racing for years. He lived alone in El Cerrito/Oakland, sometimes he arrived at a boat race in an old Roadster pulling a gated box trailer with a boat sitting atop a mattress and the motor thrown in the cockpit. He was middle age, heavy man who said he was a retired navy veteran.

SECOND HEAT

Orville's folks had come to California the hard way. Father had grown up in a Central Ohio and had married a local girl after serving in the Civil War. He had spent a few years learning to be a carpenter, then a contractor. Not satisfied with the living and economic conditions in Ohio, they decided to go west to California. They heard the great story's of gold and climate. They were young, strong and in good health.

First, down to Texas. Not too bad, mostly by boat down to New Orleans, the a relatively short trip to Texas. East Texas was too hot/humid so they tried the area around Austin, then San Antonio. Each had both attractions and problems. The pull of California was ever in mind, so off they went to New Mexico/Arizona via rail, horse/wagon and at last into Yuma through the use of a covered wagon with a US Calvary troop escort.

Yuma wasn't quite what they expected. However, it was tolerable. Weather was terribly hot in summer, but with little or no humidity. Along the Colorado River, the summer temperature at midnight tended to be warmer than the open desert, due to some humidity.

Many homes, public/commercial buildings now standing in the Yuma area, Brawley and El Centro where built at the hand of Charles Brisbin. After a few years, the family decided to move north, to the Napa Valley. Splendid reports told of this small utopian valley in the San Francisco Bay area, where folks were creating a flourishing wine industry in the ideal climate.

At that time, 1902, Napa was not an easy destination. It was rural, just beginning a dramatic growth. It is located north of San Francisco, in a little valley formed by the Sonoma mountain range on the west and protected from the San Joaquin summer heat by a small mountain range on the east side. The Napa River, had carved this small valley which empties into the San Francisco Bay.

The Brisbin family moved north. They at last had found the place which fulfilled their dream. "I thought a trip to Texas would take me back over the route my folks had traveled to bring me to California." Their experience, of course, had been hazardous and filled with adventure, this trip would be an excursion paved by a generation of travelers and businessmen.

"I drove to Marysville where we packed our gear in the 1938 Oldsmobile and boat trailer. When I asked Harold why he had decided on the 4-60 outfit rather than his PR-SC runabout or hydro, he said, "the

4-60 is the only motor I have any confidence in and the only motor I have had a chance to tune since I got out of the Army." This made sense, he knew Ashley had been mustered out of the Army

SECOND HEAT

only a short time before and was only now getting around to even thinking about boat racing. He had, prior to the war, a successful plumbing business in the Sacramento Valley and was working hard to restore the business.

"We left Marysville about noon and headed south on Highway 99. At that time, 99 was the major highway north and south and it intersected a town about every 20 miles (about the distance a horse and wagon could travel in a reasonable amount of time.) The road connected small farm villages and was the main commercial channel for all custom and commerce.

Consequently, they were typically laid out in a formal grid, in contrast to the Eastern US where a town simply followed an ancient cow-path pattern system. Each town, with its auto stop lights, general traffic, pedestrians, etc. slowed our progress down to Bakersfield.

We had a late lunch/dinner there then took Highway 58 over the Tehachapi Mountains to Barstow and Needles on the Colorado River. We got into Needles about midnight, temperature was about 90 degrees. The desert may cool off at night, but the humidity along the river allows the temperature to remain high.

We had traveled about 500 miles and I noticed a pattern for the trip. Every 100 miles required a stop for 10 gallons of gas and 1 quart of oil. This was not a burden in cost, but it resulted in the loss of time. It was with some chagrin that I asked Harold about the car and its condition. He said that the Old's was about worn out, but was the only thing he could quickly obtain after his Army discharge. He said the engine probably had a burned piston and most of the rings shot, because the motor certainly did use oil. I agreed, it did use a bit of oil!

"We got into New Mexico where I suggested we stop and get some rest. The vehicle had begun to wobble when either Harold or Jack drove, and I did think that the heat waves did seem to be getting larger. We got into Texas the next day. Dempey seemed to think we were almost to Brownwood. I had looked at the map, but really did not realize that Texas was THAT big. On and on, two lane road, little traffic, every 100 miles 10 gallons gas and one quart of oil."

Brownwood seemed to be about in the middle of Texas, above Austin, south of Abilene, between San Angelo and Waco. The race course was located on Brownwood Lake, which fed into the Colorado River (not the big Colorado of the far west.)

At the regatta, Ashley quickly found that his pre-war 4-60 and conventional Rockholt hydro was not competitive with most of his rivals who had switched to the 3pt hydro design. There were a few

SECOND HEAT

who had switched over to the 4-60 pumper. The pumper powerhead was probably a little faster, after a few modifications. The flywheel was lightened, gear ratio changed to 13:16 and the rotary valve probably tweaked.

There were a few more boats than the legal 12, so an elimination heat was necessary. Harold placed about 9-10th in that heat. He qualified, but just!

One could see that Harold was unhappy with the situation. On the west coast prior to the war he had been a consistent winner, it was probably difficult for a substantial ego to be just good enough to fill the field.

"Dempsey and I held the transom at the start of the first heat. At the 3 minute gun, Ashley continued to twirl his starting cord…at the 1 minute, he continued the routine. Dempsey got nervous at 30 seconds, said "you better start cranking Harold!" He did, the motor refused to start, he missed the heat."

The same thing occurred in the second heat. He refused to start cranking and the heat started with him swearing at the 4-60.

"However, he did not seem terribly unhappy. Dempsey was appalled, I was curious. This was not the first time I had encountered a strange personality. It seemed that Ashley took a good look at his competition and knew that his equipment was not good enough to win and he tanked rather than give it a college try. He could justify a poor performance solely on the equipment, not his competitive spirit. It was OK by me, I was only along for the ride!

I was concerned about the return trip to California. However I need not to have worried, Ashley quickly recovered, his attitude changed to a "what the hell". Not sweetness and light, but no gloom and doom.

On the trip back, the two treated me rather well, for they seemed to run out of cash and looked to me to finance the last few hundred miles on 10 gallons of gas and 1 quart of oil.

The trip was not a loss, I learned that Texas is BIG…and that a first character impression can be a big mistake."

SECOND HEAT

This & That

Random Thoughts from the Boatshop:

"This will never do!" (Probably the most famous book review ever written, Francis Jeffery 1773-1850)

*****

"There are few hours in life more agreeable than the hour dedicated to the ceremony known as afternoon tea" Henry James 1843-1916

*****

Praise like gold and diamonds owes its value only to its society" Samuel Johnson 1700-1784

*****

"A man's an awful coward when his pants begin to go" Henry Lawson 1867-1922

*****

"There is nothing more difficult to take in hand, more perilous to conduct, or more uncertain in its success than to take the load in the introduction of a new order of things" (The Prime) Niccola Machiavelli 1469-1527

*****

"I cannot tell how the truth may be: I say the tale as twas told to me" Sir Walter Scott 1776-1832

SECOND HEAT

*****

"When to the sessions of sweet silent thought I summon up remembrance of things past, I sigh the lack of many a thing I sought" (Sonnet 30, The Rope of Lacrece) William Shakespeare 1564-1616

******

"A hen is only an egg's way of making another egg" Samuel Butler 1835-1922

******

"I cannot sing the old songs now. It's not that I deem them low; tis that I can't remember how they go" Charles Calverly 1821-1894

*****

"No matter how you slice it, it's still baloney" Alfred Smith 1873-1944

******

"All the historical books which contain no lies are extremely tedious" Anatole France 1844-1924

******

"It's easy 'nough to titter w'en da stew is smoking hot; But hit's mighty ha'd to giggle w'en dey's nuffin in da pot" Paul Dunbar 1872-1959

******

SECOND HEAT

"Kilroy was here"

*****

"Lili Marlene" Germany 1938, Norbert Schultz, Haus Leit, Lala Anderson (singer, Sweden)

*****

"That's all there is; there isn't anymore" Ethel Barrymore 1879-1959

SECOND HEAT

SECOND HEAT

SECOND HEAT

SECOND HEAT

Order form

Please print names and address legibly.

Number of copies _____ ($_____) Cash/Check ($29.95 per copy)

Shipping _____ (please include $3.00 per copy for shipping and handling)

Total_____

Ship to Address

Name:_____

Address:_____

City/State:_____

Zip Code_____

Phone_____

Send this form and payment to:
Ralph DeSilva
P.O. Box 1296
Hiram Georgia 30132

www.ingramcontent.com/pod-product-compliance
Lightning Source LLC
Chambersburg PA
CBHW081200230426
43666CB00016B/2870